QuickBooks Online 2025 Handbook

A Step-By-Step Guide to Streamlining Your Company's Finances with Simple Payroll, Sales Tax, Expense, and Invoicing Management

Tim Elvis

CHAPTER ONE
QUICKBOOKS ONLINE 2025 INTRODUCTION

Intuit is the company that develops and markets the accounting software application QuickBooks. Originally introduced in 1992, QuickBooks products are mostly intended for small and medium-sized businesses. These consist of on-premises accounting applications, cloud-based accounting software, and bill management and payment solutions. A "double-entry" accounting application was not included of Quickens' initial software. QuickBooks was first made available as a DOS version, based on the Quicken codebases. In-House Accountant, a program that Intuit had acquired, served as the source of the unique codebase that the Mac and Windows versions utilized. The application was quite popular with small company owners who had no professional accounting background. As a result, the application rapidly increased its market share to 85% of the US small company accounting software market. In September 2005, QuickBooks accounted for 74% of the US market. The NPD Group said that as of March 2008, QuickBooks' retail unit share in the business accounting category has increased to 94.2 percent, citing an Intuit press release dated June 19, 2008. It also claims that more than 50,000 people, including independent business consultants, certified public accountants, and accountants, are members of the QuickBooks ProAdvisor program. In his eight years as CEO, Steve Bennett had almost tripled Intuit's sales and quadrupled its profits, but by then, Brad Smith had taken control. It continued to control a significant portion of this market as of 2013. Professional accountants, however, were not satisfied with the system's first versions, pointing up problems with insufficient security measures (such the lack of an audit trail) and non-adherence to accepted accounting standards. It's also crucial to remember that Intuit has integrated a number of web-based features into QuickBooks, including improved email functionality with Microsoft Outlook and Outlook Express, remote access capabilities, electronic payment features, online banking and reconciliation, and mapping capabilities via Google Maps integration. For the 2008 edition, the firm has included pre-authorization of electronic money, new Help tools, more employee time tracking options, and import from Excel spreadsheets. In June 2007, Intuit announced that QuickBooks Enterprise Solutions will now run on Linux servers instead of the Windows server that was previously required for it to function.

QuickBooks Online: What is it?

Another cloud service offered by Intuit is QuickBooks Online. The user subscribes to a monthly service rather than paying a one-time fee, and they can only access the program by safely checking in using a web browser. Intuit not only provides fixes and updates the application automatically, but it also inserts pop-up ads for additional commercial services within the program. In terms of online accounting solutions, Xero claimed 284,000 users as of July 2014, while QuickBooks Online had 624,000 users as of May 2014. The QuickBooks cloud edition is a distinct product since many of its features function differently from those in the desktop version.

QuickBooks Online is compatible with Internet Explorer 10, Chrome, Firefox, Safari 6.1, and Chrome for Android and Safari on iOS 7. QuickBooks Online may also be accessed via an iPhone, BlackBerry, and Android web app. In 2011, Intuit introduced a UK-specific version of QuickBooks Online to address the distinct VAT and European tax framework. There are versions designed for the Australian, Canadian, and Indian markets in addition to a worldwide version that the user may modify. QuickBooks Online offers integration with a range of financial services and third-party software, including as banks, payroll providers, and expense management software. Additionally, QuickBooks Desktop has a migration feature that lets customers transfer desktop data from Pro or Prem SKUs to QuickBooks Online.

An overview of the cloud-based financial management application QuickBooks Online

One cloud-based financial management tool is QuickBooks Online. **It is designed to help you spend less time keeping an eye on your company's finances by helping you with things like:**

+ **Creating estimates and invoices:** With QuickBooks Online, users can easily and quickly produce professional estimates and invoices for their company. This tool helps businesses maintain accurate records of their sales interactions and makes invoicing easier.
+ **Cash flow and sales tracking:** QuickBooks Online allows businesses to effectively manage cash flow and monitor sales. Users may examine their income streams and make educated financial choices by using the software's tools for recording and categorizing sales transactions.
+ Entering your bank information, creating expenses, and paying bills
+ **Expense Management:** QuickBooks Online allows users to efficiently monitor and manage their expenses. It includes features for monitoring and managing expenditure, uploading receipts, and making expense reports. This helps businesses keep a careful eye on their spending and find areas where they may cut costs.

- Making tax returns and keeping track of your taxes more simpler
- Comprehending the functioning of your business
- Budgeting and planning
- **Bank Reconciliation:** The program simplifies bank reconciliation by automatically importing and classifying bank transactions. Businesses may easily compare their bank records and financial data with the use of this feature, ensuring accuracy and reducing the likelihood of errors.
- **Analyzing and Reporting:** QuickBooks Online offers a variety of reporting alternatives to help businesses comprehend their financial performance. Users may construct personalized financial reports, including balance sheets and profit and loss statements that provide a comprehensive view of their company's financial health.
- **Cooperation and Incorporation:** QuickBooks Online facilitates seamless collaboration and communication with a range of business tools and services. Users may invite their accountants or other team members to see and work on the financial data simultaneously in order to promote productivity and collaboration.

There is no need to install any software since it is an authentic cloud service. On any computer or web-enabled device, you can access QuickBooks Online straight from your web browser, no matter where you are. All things considered, QuickBooks Online is a comprehensive financial management application that facilitates effective collaboration among businesses, streamlines finance-related tasks, reconciles bank transactions, tracks sales and costs, and generates useful reports.

Technology solutions are essential for contemporary enterprises

Look about you. Our current world differs from the one in which we were born. Over the last several years, technology has changed how we live, work, buy, communicate, and do business. It has become a part of our everyday lives and is now a necessary part of life. The importance of technology in business cannot be overstated. Businesses all around the world are relying on emerging technologies to strengthen their competitive advantage and advance their strategies and growth. It's almost impossible to operate these days without the Internet, video conferencing, project management software, and other technologies. The truth is that technology will continue to advance in the commercial world. This reality compels you to include technology into your operations, if you haven't already. Now is the moment to become acquainted with technology, and here's how to accomplish it.

Here are some justifications on why technology is so crucial to businesses:

Communication

Technology has made it possible to communicate more efficiently, swiftly, and extensively. This will include interactions with your staff, clients, potential clients, investors, and the public at large. Holding meetings from multiple places is made simple by video conferencing technologies like Zoom and Skype. Using an app like Asana or Slack might help your team communicate more efficiently about your business. Both in-person and remote workers may use this to keep track of projects, task details, deadlines, and other information. Email, newsletters, social media, and other platforms are all equally vital communication tools.

Safety

Given the rise in cybercrime and data breaches, strict security is crucial for all businesses. Most of the company's assets are now stored in the cloud or on endpoints. As a result, companies must now take strict measures to safeguard their own data as well as that of their customers. By using corporate IT solutions, you may increase the security of the data in your organization. With losses to the typical small firm expected to exceed $3.92 million, network security threats are at an all-time high. Setting up firewalls and encryptions to increase data security might be aided by small company tech support. Modern IT architecture allows businesses to replace outdated legacy systems with cloud storage choices. Cloud storage systems are reliable and provide for regulated access to company data from any place worldwide. It enables your staff to collaborate remotely and get the necessary data. By eliminating the need to run big servers, it also saves money and space.

Effectiveness

Technology increases the efficiency of systems, products, and services. It makes data flow, process monitoring and optimization, and contact and staff record administration easier. This increased operational effectiveness reduces costs and enables rapid business growth. Small and medium-sized organizations may operate as efficiently as bigger ones by using digital technologies. Key tasks may be completed more efficiently with the use of automation software and fast internet. Automation technology may help you communicate with clients more effectively and increase your online exposure.

Assistance for employees

Most workers feel obligated to utilize the newest technology while doing their duties because they believe it will allow them to provide the best results. Businesses must consider the cost-output relationship and provide suitable technology in order to enhance results. Businesses may now better organize their workforces thanks to significant advancements in communication technology. Software programs like Asana and G Suite improve employee collaboration. VOIP systems, conference calls, and telepresence software allow employees to virtually interact from any location in the world. It boosts the operational efficiency of businesses and promotes a better work-life balance.

Money and time

Without a doubt, technology allows businesses to do more tasks in less time without compromising the quality of their products or services. In reality, technology now performs repetitive tasks that were formerly performed by humans. This lowers the expense of recruiting staff or deploying them to areas where they are most required. Businesses need to be well-versed in technological tools in order to maximize their use. Information management systems assist firms monitor data, sales, production, and expenses. Data may highlight issues that need attention in addition to opportunities for improvement. Companies with strong information systems management skills will be able to innovate, save operational costs, grow into new markets, improve customer service, and outperform their competitors. With the use of business technology solutions, corporate leaders may generate new sources of income for their organizations. By creating e-commerce websites, sales teams may reach a wider audience. 2019 saw a 14% growth in consumer expenditure with US online merchants, totaling $601.75 billion. Businesses are also using the advantages of PPC and SEO marketing to boost leads and sales. Business and corporate leaders are adopting Infrastructure as a Service, outsourcing much of their IT solutions to consulting companies. The market for managed services was projected to be worth $170 billion by 2019. By using communication tools like voice-over-internet protocol and video conferencing, businesses may reduce their travel and accommodation costs. Data storage costs are reduced via cloud services. Automation reduces the demand for additional workers, which lowers labor expenses.

What's Latest in QuickBooks Online 2025?

Did you know that several creative ideas have led to a major overhaul of QuickBooks online? Let's take a moment to appreciate new discoveries and advancements that simplify a process. Below, these enhancements provide a number of time-saving recommendations!

Important improvements and additions to QuickBooks Online 2025

Using Commerce to streamline order administration and visibility

With the new inventory tools in QuickBooks Online Plus and QuickBooks Online Advanced, you can use automated accounting across sales channels to expedite order processing and inventory management. The Product and Services page in Plus and Advanced also gives you a clearer view of all your products and variations, including price and stock details. You will be notified when stock levels are low, allowing you to quickly place purchase orders to restock. Along with learning about the top-selling products and cross-channel sales patterns, you'll also be able to keep an eye on new orders coming in from other sales channels. You can observe profitability and always know where your money is going by automating reports that track the expenses of your products. Additionally, you may relax knowing that expenditure payments will be immediately reflected in your records. In conclusion, this edition will assist you in managing orders, inventory, and accounting with ease by providing a unified, useful platform designed for e-commerce businesses.

Examine more methods for batch-reclassifying transactions

Instead of opening each transaction individually and making changes by hand, you and your accountant may simply alter a whole batch of one kind of bank transaction, such a deposit or cost. In addition to accountants, company owners may now access batch adjustments with this edition, which allows you to change additional components of a bank transaction.

+ Choose Bank Transactions to start batch-editing bank transactions in fewer steps.

✛ Next, choose Categorized.

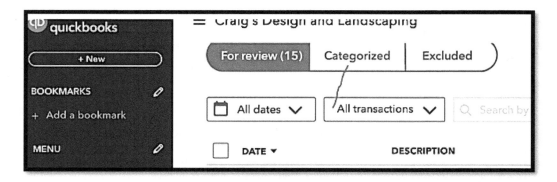

In short, you and your accountant now have a powerful tool at your disposal that lets you reclassify additional bank transaction characteristics in bulk.

Workflows may have numerous approvers added

Regardless of your company's structure, you will be able to set up the bill approval process so that invoices are sent to all pertinent parties prior to payment. Additionally, you can keep an eye on and review an audit trail of these approvals in real time throughout and after the operation. In short, a number of criteria have been added to the QuickBooks Online Advanced Workflows function. Your advanced procedures may now include several consecutive approvers for invoices that meet the precise criteria you specified.

Increased App Control

Any principal administrator on a QuickBooks subscription may now unlink apps that were linked by other subscribers. Previously, main administrators could only examine applications that were linked via other admins' admins. You may now focus on the applications you rely on by choosing Disconnect to remove any unwanted or superfluous apps from the list. In short, company owners now have more control over which apps are connected to QuickBooks Online.

Fresh KPI information for your company

To highlight certain KPIs, you may choose from a few additional widgets on your homepage or company overview. You may better understand your company's performance and financial health by gaining new insights.

Some of the new widgets are as follows:
- **Mileage:** gathers and enters into QuickBooks Online the mileage that customers log when traveling for business. Only the mobile edition of QuickBooks Online included this widget.
- **Accounts Payable:** enumerates all of your business's immediate debts and commitments to vendors and suppliers.
- The sums that your business has invoiced but not yet received are shown in accounts receivable.
- Select Customize layout to add a new widget, and then Widgets may be added or removed.

In conclusion, you have more options than ever before for keeping an eye on your business's performance.

Payroll items may be assigned to many workers simultaneously

Instead of changing employee data from their profiles, you may complete more tasks in fewer stages by choosing Edit Payroll Items on the Employees tab:
- See every kind of compensation, deduction, and contribution that an employee has been allotted.
- See the list of employees assigned to each pay item.
- Use a simple way to assign many employees to each pay item.
- Arrange employees according on their kind, position, and workplace.
- Change several workers' assignment information at once.

In conclusion, QuickBooks Payroll has made it simple to generate and allocate payroll items to many workers.

Using a keyboard shortcut, launch QuickBooks Payroll

After logging into QuickBooks to process payroll, you don't have to spend time navigating between pages to reach the Payroll page.

+ You may start paying your employees by simply pressing Ctrl + Alt/Option + "u" to start the payroll process.

Footnote: To see all of the shortcuts that are accessible, use Ctrl + Alt/Option + Command/Windows key + "/".

In conclusion, you may now save time by using a keyboard shortcut to do payroll in QuickBooks Online from any place.

Get Allstate Health Solutions by using Online Payroll in QuickBooks

QuickBooks Payroll customers may now easily acquire a variety of affordable, customizable healthcare solutions via the Benefits page. Allstate Health Solutions offers more than 200 regional and national health insurance carriers. Additionally, you may purchase dental and vision insurance to enhance your coverage at no extra cost. If you choose a package, QuickBooks will manage and seamlessly integrate your payroll deductions. You may apply for coverage, compare plans, and look into health savings options with the assistance of a dedicated team of professionals at Allstate Health Solutions. They'll make sure you receive the ongoing support you need both while you're weighing your choices and after you've enrolled. In conclusion, if your business does not presently provide health benefits to its employees, it may be challenging to choose and execute the best plan. To expedite this process, we are thrilled to announce our partnership with Allstate Health Solutions.

Inform a client of their outstanding amounts

Prior to this update, your customers would get separate email reminders for each invoice, making it difficult for them to locate and remember to pay each one.

+ To send a grouped reminder to a client, choose Sales first, followed by Customers.
+ In the Action column for your client, choose Send Reminder.
+ Follow the instructions on the website to inform your client of all their unpaid debts.

Use QuickBooks Payments to send invoices together with SMS messages

- To access this functionality, you must be a U.S.-based Payments merchant and submit pay-enabled invoices on the Rethink platform.
- You have the option to include an SMS message when your invoice has been received and approved. After that, you may modify the text message preview and add your customer's cellphone number if needed. After that, choose Send Invoice to email and text your customer the invoice.

Footnote: Get your customer's permission before texting them an invoice.

In conclusion, if you use QuickBooks Payments, you can now send text messages to your customers in addition to email invoices. By raising awareness of them, this might make it easier for your customers to pay their invoices.

Journal entries from a batch import

To send in one or more CSV files with journal entries, each with up to 1,000 rows of data— select Journal entries from the Import data menu.

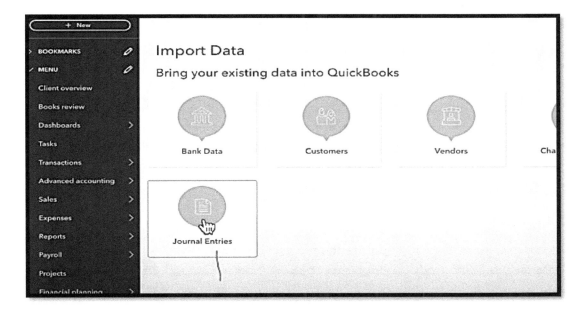

Following the Settings selection:

In summary: You may now import journal entries into QuickBooks Online in bulk without the need for third-party software or manual effort. Uploading diary entries rather than retyping them may also help you keep your financial data accurate and consistent.

Create transactions for items and sales receipts using a bank feed

To keep up with sales performance and compliance, manually creating transactions and matching them takes additional time and work. With QuickBooks Online, you can now use your bank feed to add transactions to the books at a more detailed item level. Transactions may also be included as sales receipts for better classification. Additionally, QuickBooks Online Advanced allows you to build an estimate versus the real report by separating transactions from the bank feed by product or service. In summary, you may now conduct transactions straight from your bank feed to improve reporting and get a better understanding of your company's performance.

For a 1.5% charge, rapidly transfer QuickBooks Checking money to an outside bank

Even when you have scheduled payments in your external bank account, you may want to utilize the funds in your QuickBooks Checking account to pay bills, payroll, or other costs immediately. The several days it takes for ACH to conduct a transaction might be problematic for your business, which is already short on finances. You can now avoid that waiting time by quickly transferring funds from QuickBooks Checking to your external bank for a 1.5% charge. Comparing its many versions with QuickBooks Desktop, the four basic plans that QuickBooks Online provides are Simple Start, Essentials, Plus, and Advanced. These plans have monthly costs ranging from $30 to $200. They are made to fulfill different purposes, thus their features and user bases vary. Meanwhile, QuickBooks Solopreneur, a more sophisticated version of QuickBooks Self-Employed, is designed for one-person businesses and costs $20 a month. However, existing customers who are Self-Employed might choose to renew their contracts. For new users, QuickBooks Solopreneur is a smart choice.

Solopreneur

Entrepreneurs who need to separate their personal and business expenses: QuickBooks Solopreneur automatically distinguishes between personal and business expenses for taxes reasons. **It helps you avoid financial mixing and accurately record deductible business expenses.**

+ **Project-based consultants and freelancers:** QuickBooks Solopreneur may be used to send invoices to customers and keep track of expenses.
+ **Self-Employed QuickBooks** has become outdated for independent contractors. If you need more features, such as the ability to create and submit estimates and

monitor and record expenditures, it may be time to switch to QuickBooks Solopreneur.

+ **Solopreneur entrepreneurs that travel frequently:** QuickBooks Solopreneur has an integrated mileage tracker that lets you keep track of the miles you travel for work and use the data to claim tax reimbursement.

Easy Start

+ **Small company regular payment plans:** Simple Start offers additional features than QuickBooks Solopreneur, including the ability to set up subscriptions and recurring payments. This makes it ideal for consumers who have monthly bills that don't change, like rent, utilities, or subscription fees.
+ **Small businesses with employees:** Through its interface with QuickBooks Payroll, Simple Start helps you with payroll-related tasks including processing paychecks and calculating payroll taxes.
+ **Businesses that pay employees or suppliers using checks:** To pay for expenditures and employee compensation, you may use Solopreneur to input and print checks.

The Essentials

Essentials is superior than Simple Start in the following circumstances, however it works best for businesses with employees and clients that pay by check:
+ **Small businesses with three or fewer users:** Adding up to three users when using Essentials does not incur additional fees.
+ **Businesses that are required to keep an eye on past-due invoices:** Unlike Simple Start and Solopreneur, Essentials allows you to manage and pay supplier and vendor expenses. You may also keep a watch on overdue invoices to manage your accounts payable (A/P).
+ **Companies that provide services and bill clients on an hourly basis:** Essentials allows you to monitor billable hours by client and project. The software allows for the instant entry and documentation of employee hours spent on projects.
+ **Those who do business with other countries:** The plan's flexibility for other currencies makes it suitable for those who do business outside of the US.

The Plus

All of Essentials' features are included in plus, however plus is superior for:
+ Companies with five or less people: We believe that QuickBooks Online's most popular plan, plus, will provide access for up to five users for the majority of small firms.

- Businesses with inventory: Since Plus allows you to keep an eye on inventory and COGS; it's an essential tool for businesses that sell goods.
- With capabilities like the ability to create and oversee projects, allocate resources to them, and monitor costs, salaries, and other expenditures associated with each project, plus is another resource for businesses searching for project management solutions.
- Businesses having many sites and divisions: Businesses with various departments or segments or those operating in different locations may find the class and location monitoring features of QuickBooks Online Plus useful. For instance, HVAC (heating, ventilation, and air conditioning) businesses may use classes to monitor the income and expenses associated with each of their services, such as maintenance, repair, and installation.

Advanced

Although it offers all of the Plus plan's features and capabilities, we recommend it in particular for:

- **SMBs with up to 25 users:** Advanced allows up to 25 users, in contrast to Plus's five-user limit.
- Advanced provides the capability to register and monitor fixed assets, as well as to automatically calculate depreciation, establish depreciation schedules, and produce fixed asset reports for companies who need to keep track of their fixed assets.
- **Businesses with multiple entities:** Advanced now allow you to combine financial data from multiple business files into a single report.
- Companies that need to monitor project costs, both estimated and actual, may find the actual vs. project cost reports useful as they will help you better understand the profitability of each project you work on.
- **Businesses with complex accounting procedures:** If your company has complex financial procedures and you want your employees to fully exploit QuickBooks Online's features, Advanced offers complimentary training worth $3,000.

Comparing QuickBooks Desktop and QuickBooks Online

I found that QuickBooks Online was far more efficient, modern, and easy to use than QuickBooks Desktop throughout my testing. Every step of the procedure started with a lecture that asked me specific questions to help me create my company's profile. Simply said, QuickBooks Desktop was slow. I was reminded of the dial-up tone on my family's

Pentium III computer in 1998 by everything about it, including the installation page and the sluggish user interface. Although there were less tutorial-style prompts, the sheer number of functionality was still a nice surprise to me. **Some of the many factors that distinguish QuickBooks desktop from QuickBooks online are listed below:**

- While QuickBooks Desktop is installed locally, QuickBooks Online may be accessed from any device with an internet connection: QuickBooks Online is the cloud-based option. All you need is your account information to access your QuickBooks records on any internet-connected device. Suppose you have a global workforce that completes QuickBooks remotely from different places. In this case, QuickBooks Online would be the better option. QuickBooks Desktop, on the other hand, may be downloaded and installed locally on one or more computers in your workplace. Once installed, your accounting data will only be accessible on one of these devices, making it difficult to work while on the road. But with the local installation, you have more control over who can access your data and how safe it is for the information of your business as a whole.

- While QuickBooks Desktop provides additional options for individual users, QuickBooks Online allows for more collaboration: Fastness is critical for many teams. If your accounting software doesn't immediately capture changes, it might lead to costly delays. QuickBooks Online is excellent in this area. By facilitating multi-user access to accounting data, it aims to promote user collaboration. Each user has their own login credentials, which may be changed to limit access to personal information. There is also a function that facilitates inviting your accountant to utilize the website and gives them instant access to your data. The goal of QuickBooks Online is to make it as simple as possible to use and navigate. The side menu's features are conveniently arranged by category. For example, components pertaining to workers, their taxes, and compliance data are grouped under the Payroll category. A quick tour is more than enough to familiarize oneself with the capabilities that QuickBooks Online provides, even if it takes some time to explore and get a feel for where everything is. Another noteworthy feature of QuickBooks Online is its AI assistant tool. It helps with email creation, offers accounting insights, and enables message auto-drafting. I awarded it two stars because, unlike QuickBooks Desktop, it actually exists, even if I believe it to be a quite simple AI tool. QuickBooks Desktop has more features that provide you a comprehensive view of your accounting procedures, even if it does not have the same multi-user accessibility. QuickBooks Desktop offers more advanced inventory management features, sales orders, project costing spreadsheets, and fully configurable reports. I was astounded to learn that you could conduct batch invoicing, which is not supported by QuickBooks Online.

- Unlike QuickBooks Online, QuickBooks Desktop has fewer integration options: The issue with accounting programs like QuickBooks Desktop is that they are designed to run locally and independently, which leaves limited room for interaction with other programs, especially ones housed in the cloud. Similar to how iOS and Apple devices seemed when everyone had hot, self-cooking Android phones, QuickBooks Desktop may feel rigid and unyielding, making it difficult to integrate or modify. Implementation is challenging due to the product. This is where QuickBooks Online shines; the applications tab has a search bar and applications that you may connect to improve analytical and reporting capabilities, such as managing revenue and spending, time tracking, invoicing, and client administration. Additionally, Zapier and QuickBooks Online may be linked, enabling you to connect QuickBooks to hundreds of other applications in your business's IT stack. You can automatically add customers to QuickBooks and print receipts when payments are made in other applications, or you can monitor new QuickBooks invoices or payments in another app. These pre-made routines will give you a sense of what's available, but you can use Zapier to connect QuickBooks to almost any application you use.
- Compared to QuickBooks Desktop, QuickBooks Online is lighter, quicker, and uses less processing power: Despite my fond childhood recollections of technology and my twelve years of playing "PLAYER 2," I don't miss how slow it was in the past. You should anticipate short loading times even if QuickBooks Desktop may not meet your expectations in terms of contemporary technologies. Since it is installed software on your local system, it is reliant on the resources and processing power of the device. For more complex processes or bigger datasets, QuickBooks Desktop could need more local computing power than the online version. Nevertheless, Intuit owns the servers that host QuickBooks Online. Since it is a cloud-based technology, its interface is a web page. It provides quicker load times and response rates while using less local processing power. On any laptop that deserved the moniker, it would function flawlessly.

QuickBooks Online 2025: Who Needs It?

Benefits and target audience for various user categories

The many target markets for QuickBooks online are discussed in this section, along with the range of advantages it provides to different user groups.

- **Small Company Owners:** QuickBooks Online is designed to make managing finances easier for small company owners. It facilitates the creation of invoices, payroll organization, and expenditure tracking. The following benefits are provided by QuickBooks Online to this target audience: a user-friendly interface that eliminates the need for in-depth accounting knowledge when managing money; it quickly generates and distributes expert invoices; and it tracks cash flow to ensure the company has a steady financial position.

- **Independent Contractors and Self-Employed Professionals:** QuickBooks Online assists self-employed professionals and independent contractors in tracking their expenses and income, managing their travel, and estimating their taxes. **The following are the benefits for this target audience:**
  - ➢ Keep detailed records of each transaction. Filing taxes is made simpler by estimated tax payments and structured financial data. Create invoices and accept payments online.
- **Bookkeepers and accountants:** Bookkeepers and accountants utilize QuickBooks Online to guarantee accurate accounting, generate reports, and speed up their customers' financial transactions. **QuickBooks Online offers the following benefits to this target market:**
  - ➢ They need to safely access client accounts in order to manage their books. Create comprehensive financial reports and effortlessly integrate accounting software with other business tools.
- **Medium-Sized Enterprises:** Medium-sized businesses utilize QuickBooks Online to do more complex financial tasks including payroll processing, managing many users, and connecting with other company tools. **Benefits include of**
  - ➢ More advanced technologies are being made available to assist growing companies and handle wage and tax reporting. Keep an eye on project expenses and profitability, as well as stock levels and inventory.
- **Entrepreneurs:** QuickBooks Online helps entrepreneurs properly manage their finances from the beginning, allowing them to grow and expand. Among the benefits QuickBooks provides for this goal are
  - ➢ To be ready for growth, start organizing your finances early on and make budgets and financial predictions. Make financial reports available to potential investors. Sustain a robust cash flow to support the phases of growth.

Why QuickBooks Online Is Better Than Desktop

Collaboration and real-time access

In my view, this is one of the most important traits. For a corporate file, QBO allows users to use the program from any place and on many devices. All you have to do is go to the QBO website and log in. This feature allows several users and corporate locations to access the application, without the need for extra software. Additionally, QBO allows several users to utilize the application at the same time. This is really helpful if you have a bookkeeper and work with an outsourced accounting firm like The Quantify Group. While we were both enrolled in the QBO program, I had previously taught bookkeepers for a number of companies. This saved us a great deal of time and money since we could do quick or even lengthy training remotely.

Integration with other applications and scalability

QuickBooks Online offers a variety of subscription levels that may grow with your business. You may begin with basic features and progress to more complex options as required. QuickBooks Online provides advanced features including enhanced inventory management, more comprehensive reporting, and robust payroll tools in response to expanding company demands. Additionally, it allows businesses to add additional employees as their team grows since access privileges can be adjusted to ensure data protection. Additionally, it interfaces with several third-party applications to provide smooth data transfer and synchronization between platforms, reducing the likelihood of mistakes and manual data entry. By centralizing financial data and integrating it with other corporate technology, QuickBooks Online improves the precision and effectiveness of financial management. Connects to payment gateways such as PayPal, Stripe, and Square to make transaction processing and payment reconciliation easier. Its interface with CRM solutions, such as Salesforce and HubSpot, which link financial data to customer interactions and sales activities, enables better customer relationship management. QuickBooks Online's scalability ensures that businesses can develop without outgrowing their accounting application and the many connectors enhance the platform's functionality, speed up procedures, and promote better decision-making. These advantages make QuickBooks Online a powerful and flexible choice for a variety of user types, including small and medium-sized enterprises.

Backups and upgrades that happen automatically

Numerous QBO systems allow for automated transaction processing. The first is a steady flow of credit card and bank transactions that are created automatically. This feed allows for specific transaction customization, such as allocating expenses across accounts and business sectors, and it will automatically repeat each time. Second, QBO provides a number of automated services for customer billing, email reporting, and payroll. Additionally, Intuit provides corporate file backups and scheduled software upgrades. Companies may upload documents to QBO and link them to specific transactions, saving them a lot of money on costly paperless document storage. This will please your accountant as well. He or she will always have access to supporting evidence to lower your taxes.

Practice Exercises

- What is Online QuickBooks?
- How crucial are technology solutions to contemporary business?
- Who is the target market for QuickBooks online?
- How does QuickBooks Online differ from QuickBooks Desktop?

CHAPTER TWO
QUICKBOOKS ONLINE2025 CONFIGURATIONS

QuickBooks Online 2025, the latest edition of Intuit's popular cloud-based accounting software, is designed to help businesses of all sizes manage their finances effectively. With its various features, this useful tool may satisfy the needs of small company owners, accountants, freelancers, and small and medium-sized enterprises. Because of its extensive feature set and user-friendly interface, QuickBooks Online 2025 is an essential tool for modern businesses trying to streamline their financial processes. This chapter will teach you how to set up the most recent version of QuickBooks efficiently. This involves setting up your business profile, creating and managing accounts, navigating the user interface, and integrating credit cards and bank accounts.

Registration and Account Management

To adjust settings for all of your products, utilize your QuickBooks user account when you wish to sign up for a new QuickBooks Online product. An email address is linked to this account. Use these procedures if you need to upgrade an existing QuickBooks user account.

Check or update your information

- Go to the Intuit Account Manager.
- To log in, enter your QuickBooks login credentials.

+ Select Sign-in & security, Profile, Data privacy, or Products & billing to examine the settings.
+ Select a field and follow the directions to make any changes.

Keep in mind: You may also access the Intuit Account Manager using QuickBooks Online by performing the following:

+ Launch QuickBooks Online, and then sign in.
+ Click the profile icon to access your Intuit account.

YOUR COMPANY	LISTS	TOOLS	PROFILE
Account and settings	All lists	Order checks	Subscriptions and billing
Manage users	Products and services	Import data	Feedback
Custom form styles	Recurring transactions	Import desktop data	Privacy
Chart of accounts	Attachments	Export data	
Get the desktop app	Custom fields	Reconcile	
Additional info	Tags	Budgeting	
	Rules	Audit log	
		SmartLook	
		Resolution center	

You're viewing QuickBooks in **Business view**. Find out more   Switch to Accountant view

To see every one of your goods

+ Go to the Intuit Account Manager.
+ To log in, enter your QuickBooks login credentials.
+ Make product and billing decisions.

Here, you may modify your product's payment information and subscription choices. Use the procedures listed below to get your data from the Intuit account manager:

+ Log in to the Intuit Account Manager after opening it.
+ Make the selection "Data privacy."
+ Select "Download."
+ Click "Continue" to confirm. On average, requests might take up to 15 days. How long it takes depends on the size of your request. You will not be able to submit any more download or delete requests during this time.

Do the following in order to examine recent activity:

+ Go to the Intuit Account Manager.
+ To log in, enter your QuickBooks login credentials.

- Select Security and log in.
- Select Account Activities.
- This shows the location of recent sign-ins. This makes it easier to see any suspicious activity on your account.

How to register for a new account on QuickBooks Online

Follow these procedures if you're a new user or would want an independent user account for yourself or your company:
- Go to the section about Intuit accounts.
- To create an account, choose Create.
- Type in your email address and phone number. Note: If the notice "This user ID is already taken" appears, it may indicate that you already have an account. Enter your email address after choosing I forgot my password or user ID.

- Create a passcode.
- Click Create account once you're ready.

I'll send you an email with a link to verify your email address. You're then prepared to go.

Recognizing various subscription plans

Whether you are a small business owner starting your first firm or moving your existing books online, you will discover a range of QuickBooks Online subscription options to meet your requirements as your company grows. Let's review each QuickBooks Online membership level and associated costs to help you choose the best QuickBooks edition for your small company. From free monthly use to the priciest subscription ($200/month for QuickBooks Advanced), QuickBooks offers a variety of options. QuickBooks Money is a free money management tool that doesn't need any accounting features or a minimum monthly balance. QuickBooks Solopreneur provides easy-to-use accounting solutions for independent contractors. Plans begin at $20 per month. There are four subscription tiers for QuickBooks Online: Simple Start costs $30, Essentials costs $60, Plus costs $90, and Advanced costs $200. Note: You may check prices on our pricing page, since they change based on the goods. There is a free 30-day trial available for QuickBooks Online plans.

The QuickBooks Money

For independent business owners looking for a single point of contact for banking and payments, QuickBooks Money is a complete financial management solution. When they register a free account, freelancers and solopreneurs may handle their money from anywhere without any monthly fees or minimum balance restrictions. With QuickBooks Money's QuickBooks Checking business bank account, you can manage your finances, submit invoices, get paid, and earn the greatest market annual percentage yield (APY) all in one place without having to subscribe. If your business needs capabilities like automated transaction matching, mileage and expenditure tracking, bill payment, receipt capturing, or professional support, QuickBooks Money is not a good fit since it does not include accounting tools. If you need accounting features, you may browse through more QuickBooks plans to get the perfect one for your business. Switching to a QuickBooks Online subscription plan from QuickBooks Money is easy. Your user profile, bank and merchant account details, bank and payment transaction history, and more are all transmitted. You also get access to all of your accounting data. Even if you want to cancel your QuickBooks Online subscription, you may still access your QuickBooks Money account and data.

QuickBooks Solopreneur

QuickBooks Solopreneur is a user-friendly version of QuickBooks made especially for one-person operations. If you are a sole owner utilizing Schedule C (form 1040), QuickBooks Solopreneur is designed for businesses like yours. With QuickBooks Solopreneur, you can run your business more efficiently, remain ready for taxes, and know how your firm is doing. QuickBooks Solopreneur is a big improvement for those who now monitor in Excel, save their receipts in shoeboxes, or don't have a way to organize their company money before submitting Schedule-C forms. Additionally, TurboTax allows you to pay just when you file, move easily from books to taxes for easier filing, and get real-time tax expert assistance. (Prices start at $169 and vary according on eligibility and the kind of business.)* QuickBooks Solopreneur plans are $20 each month. Growth- and tax-focused solutions to support financial stability are part of QuickBooks Solopreneur's simple feature set. You may use IRS materials or see an accountant if you are unclear about your filing obligations. Only sole owners that submit a Schedule C form may use QuickBooks Solopreneur. Additionally, QuickBooks Solopreneur is not a good option for small businesses with employees or those with more complex accounting needs. You may check into QuickBooks Online plans if your business requires additional features; if not, read on to learn more about the features that are part of QuickBooks Online plans.

Simple Start

The purpose of QuickBooks Online Simple Start is to support sole proprietorships, partnerships, LLCs, and other small company forms. It is the greatest choice for single users with basic accounting requirements. Simple Start plans cost $30 a month and include with all the required accounting tools. You may ask up to two accounting firms to review your records for free, but Simple Start is just for one user. Add on a QuickBooks Payroll subscription (additional costs apply) to handle payroll taxes from inside QuickBooks and pay workers and 1099 contractors via 24-hour direct deposit. When it comes time to file your taxes, TurboTax tax experts are there to help you in real time. Simply pay when you submit and take a risk-free exam. (Costs vary by entity type and start at $169. Subject to eligibility.)* Simple Start may not be appropriate for businesses that manage a large number of users, maintain inventory, create purchase orders, track billable time and expenses, handle bills (accounts payable), track projects for job costing, create budgets, deal with multiple currencies, or need more thorough reporting. If these requirements apply to your business, consider moving to a different membership tier.

Essentials

With the addition of functionality for bigger businesses, QuickBooks Online Essentials offers all the features of Simple Start. Up to three people may be granted access to QuickBooks Essentials. You may also allow employees and contractors to enter their hours using the time-tracking function. These users don't go above the three-user restriction. When each user enters their login information, QuickBooks creates a thorough audit trail that records who performs what. Essentials plans start at $60 per month. For twice as much as Simple Start, you'll receive additional users, bill administration and payment features, time tracking, the option to mark time as billable, transaction automation, multiple currency management, and twice as many reports to help you better understand your company. Additionally, you may use TurboTax to file your taxes directly from QuickBooks with the assistance of actual tax experts. Simply pay when you submit and take a risk-free exam. (Starting at $169, prices vary according on eligibility and the sort of business.) Essentials isn't a good option for anybody who has to write purchase orders, monitor projects for job costing, designate expenditure as billable, acquire, sell, and manage inventory, or create budgets. You should consider purchasing a Plus membership if your business meets these requirements.

Plus

For small companies with more complex needs, QuickBooks Online Plus delivers functionality above what is available in Simple Start and Essentials. The most popular subscription tier is this one. Plans for QuickBooks Online Plus cost $90 per month. Plus supports up to five users and lets you tailor user access. It is also possible to invite users who can just run reports; however, they are unable to make changes. These users are exempt from the five-user limit. You can add additional users, monitor transactions by location and class, manage inventory, build budgets, track tasks with Project Profitability, and receive even more information with Plus. As with earlier versions of QuickBooks Online, TurboTax allows you to electronically file your taxes from QuickBooks with the help of live tax experts. Simply pay when you submit and take a risk-free exam. (Prices start at $169 and vary based on eligibility.) QuickBooks Online Plus is not a suitable match for businesses that need to handle more than 250 active accounts, more than 40 courses and locations, or more than five employees. If your business meets these requirements, you may wish to consider becoming a subscriber to Advance.

Advanced

QuickBooks Online Advanced includes the Simple Start, Essentials, and Plus features as well as additional functionality for growing companies approaching mid-market size. QuickBooks Online Advanced costs $200 per month. Advanced can accommodate three accounting businesses and up to 25 users. User rights may be limited to 25 individuals in order to increase job delegation and visibility limitation. Another option is to invite time-tracking and reports-only users, who are exempt from the 25-user limit. Faster invoicing, the ability to track ten custom fields (Simple Start, Essentials, and Plus can only track three), access to Fathom for advanced reporting and analytics, 20 extra users, an infinite chart of accounts, class, and location lists, and Priority Circle benefits are all included in Advanced, despite the fact that it costs more than Plus. Additionally, you may use

TurboTax to file your taxes directly from QuickBooks with the assistance of actual tax experts. Simply pay when you submit and take a risk-free exam. (Starting at $169, prices vary according on eligibility and the kind of business.)

How to Use the Interface

The QuickBooks Online User Interface is the name given to the program's visual layout and design. It is the interface that users use to do a number of accounting tasks, such as handling invoices, tracking expenses, and producing financial reports. Think of the user interface as the control panel of a car. You can effectively access and manage your financial data with its many buttons and features. The QuickBooks Online User Interface makes it easy for you to monitor the financial health of your business by providing vital financial data in a timely manner, much as an automobile's dashboard does by displaying important facts like speed, fuel level, and kilometers. The user interface of QuickBooks Online is designed to be easy to use and intuitive. Accessing a range of functions and capabilities is made easy by its neatly arranged tabs, menus, and icons. For example, the QuickBooks Online User Interface makes it easy to collaborate with your accountant, create and send professional-looking invoices to customers, and manage your income and spending. The User Interface also provides real-time information and alerts to assist you in managing your finances. For instance, you may create deadline alerts, get reminders for past-due payments, and see cash flow charts to analyze your company's financial patterns. In summary, the instrument that enables customers to efficiently handle their financial responsibilities is the visually appealing and user-friendly QuickBooks Online User Interface. Its feature-rich design and user-friendly interface help businesses of all sizes remain organized, keep an eye on their money, and make informed choices.

An overview of the dashboard for QuickBooks Online

The purpose of a dashboard that is incorporated into QuickBooks Online is to provide you a concise but helpful overview of the financial status of your business. When you have access to the key indicators, you can make educated choices about your finances, inventory, and overall company strategy. The dashboard presents the data in a number of ways and displays parameters that affect your business. This includes metrics such as your previous month's profit and loss, the sums of your accounts receivable and due, and your projected invoices. There is more to the QuickBooks native dashboard than merely displaying statistics. It may alert you to problems such as past-due bills or mismatched bank transactions. With its movable layout, the dashboard is yours to personalize.

QuickBooks allows for the tracking, visualization, and reporting of key financial performance measures, but all of the representations are read-only. This suggests that there is no way to change the filters or time periods. It is crucial to keep in mind that the information downloaded from QuickBooks Online may be used to create a customized QuickBooks dashboard in BI tools or spreadsheets. All you need to do is choose the right solution, such as Looker Studio, and build a dashboard in it. Your QuickBooks data needs to be loaded. This may be done using Coupler.io, which links QuickBooks Online to data warehouses, spreadsheets, and BI tools. Another option is to purchase a readymade dashboard template. By doing this, you have an operational analytics dashboard that is prepared for the addition of your data. The latter may be finished automatically or manually if a QuickBooks Online connection is installed on the template.

Dashboard for QuickBooks Revenue

The revenue dashboard gives you a comprehensive picture of all your income sources. In addition to product and customer breakdowns, it shows the overall income for a certain time period. There is also a table with details about your bills that you may sort by date, customer, and status. Use this QuickBooks revenue dashboard to monitor revenue growth, identify top-selling products and services, and identify areas where sales might be increased. The template is compatible with Looker Studio and Power BI.

QuickBooks's Accounts Payable Dashboard

With the Accounts Payable dashboard, you can effectively manage your invoices and monitor your outgoing payments. It displays the age of accounts payable, a summary of cash and banks, and the quantity of invoices paid and unpaid by vendor. This QuickBooks dashboard makes it simple to keep an eye on your payments, preventing late penalties and promoting effective cash flow management.

QuickBooks's Accounts Receivable Dashboard

To ensure on-time collections and track incoming payments, get an accounts receivable dashboard in addition to the AP panel. This design for a QuickBooks dashboard shows the total amount of your accounts receivable, a comparison of paid and outstanding bills, and the age of your receivables. This allows you to identify debts that have been past due for a certain period of time. Use the dashboard to prioritize collections, keep track of past-due bills, and improve your cash flow in general.

An explanation of native QuickBooks dashboard analytics

Let's move back to the QuickBooks Online dashboard, which is a part of the application and provides you with an overview of all the activities that are taking place in your company. It includes a number of measures that you can use to assess your data and monitor the efficiency of your operations in a convenient manner. The dashboard is what you see when you first log into QuickBooks. If you are a new user, the dashboard's content will be blank. However, the website will be updated as soon as you start entering transactions. The interface has two tabs: Home and Cash Flow. The Home tab has a number of different widgets. By default, you may have tasks, sales, invoices, bank accounts, and shortcuts. You may add and delete widgets as you want. With the setup guide, you may set up your tax information, manage your account, and change your invoice design, among other business-related chores. You may save time on tedious tasks and browse QuickBooks features more quickly by using shortcuts. These tasks include creating a bill, adding a supplier, adding a fee, adding a new customer, and more.

The bank accounts option shows the balance for the current account you have connected to QuickBooks Online. The Cash Flow tab gives you a summary of your current cash balance, including money coming in from open and past-due invoices and money going out from open and past-due payments. Setting priorities for crucial financial data is the main objective of the integrated QuickBooks dashboard. This makes it possible for you to assess the performance of your business more quickly. By the way, the QuickBooks Online mobile app allows you to manage your accounts and access your dashboard at any time and from any location. Even though the QuickBooks Online dashboard has a pre-made set of widgets, you may rearrange them so that the most crucial information appears first. Click "b" in the top right corner of the dashboard to add or delete widgets and move them around. **You may add the following widgets to your dashboard:**

- Accounts Payable
- Accounts Receivable
- Bank Accounts
- Cashflow
- Expenses
- Invoices
- My apps
- Profit & Loss
- Sales shortcuts
- Tasks

Making your workstation more efficient

Learn how to customize QuickBooks for Mac's workspace, toolbar, tabs, and color display. If you use QuickBooks often, you may set it up to show the features that are most important to you on the default screen. This is the approach.

Configure your workplace by default

You may choose which transaction windows you want to open as soon as QuickBooks opens.
- Open a transaction window that you use often, such Write Checks.
- Select the Window option.

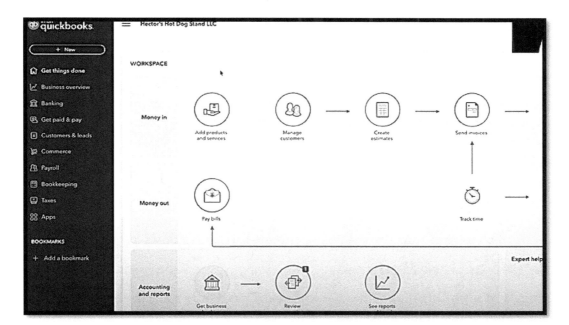

- Click Save Workspace after selecting Workspace. Do this for other transaction windows.

Personalize the toolbar in QuickBooks

You may customize your toolbar to help you with your daily QuickBooks tasks.
- To begin, choose Settings from the QuickBooks menu.
- Select the Toolbar or Tabs.

- Choose the changes you want to make; choose Display Toolbar if you want to view the toolbar while using QuickBooks. Next, decide between a display that is vertical or horizontal.
  - Choose Keep Vertical Toolbar enlarged if you want the vertical toolbar to remain enlarged at all times.
  - You may also add windows or transaction icons to the toolbar to make transactions more accessible.
- To add or delete icons, just drag & drop them into the toolbar. To reorganize them, drag them to the toolbar.
- To add a link to a transaction window in the toolbar.
  - To connect a window, first open it, and then choose Customize from the toolbar.
  - You may drag the window to the toolbar.
  - Choose an icon for the link after giving a description.

Make use of tabbed windows

Transaction windows may be set up to open as tabs in order to optimize available space.
- To begin, choose Settings from the QuickBooks menu.
- Select the Toolbar or Tabs.
- Press the "Use Tabbed Windows" button.
- **Choose the window configuration that you want to use:**
  - Select the Comparable Windows tab. to put similar windows together, such as centers, lists, registrations, forms, and reports.
  - To merge or tab every window, choose Tab All Windows in unison.

Make use of Dark Mode

For macOS Mojave (11.4) and later, QuickBooks Dark Mode is accessible.
- Select System Preferences from the Apple menu.
- After selecting General, choose Dark.

Take note: The accent color you choose for buttons and icons is used by QuickBooks.

Customize your account registrations' color

You may add some color to your account registrations to make your everyday tasks more exciting. You may do this if you are using Light or Dark Mode in QuickBooks.
- Access any account that has been registered.
- Select the color option from the dropdown menu in the top right corner. To see more options and display the color pallet, choose Other.

- Select the color you want to use for your registration. The text, rows, and registration content all use that color.
- If you do not want the text to show in the color you have chosen, pick the color ▼ option. Next, uncheck Allows Color Text.

Recognizing shortcuts and navigation menus

With the QuickBooks Online menu, you can easily access your most important work areas, like banking, staff management, invoicing, and more. You will learn about your menu and how to customize it to fit your tastes and habits.

An overview of the menu for navigating

Accounting professionals and company owners will find it simpler to navigate now that company View and Accountant View share a single menu.

- You may make your menu seem cleaner by selecting the Expand Dropdown arrow icon and Collapse menu icon for each item.
- For convenience, bookmarks are placed at the top of the menu.
- When you hover over the main menu object, all sub-menu items are shown using hover and flyout menu actions.
- Dashboards include the cash flow page, planner, and configurable home productivity center.
- You may import, categorize, and assess bank transactions and receipts using transactions. Additionally, you may monitor and reconcile your charts of accounts.
- Sales are in charge of your invoicing center and have the ability to monitor revenue over time.
- Expenses involve your expenditure activities, such as paying suppliers.
- Customers and leads are where you can create and monitor customers and use Mailchimp to promote to them.
- Reports provide you information on a number of aspects of your company. others people care about spending, others about sales, and some care about a mix of the two.
- It's via workers that you get to manage employees.
- Projects (available in Plus) let you run project-specific reports from a single dashboard and monitor profitability by project revenue, spending, and labor costs.
- Budgets (available in Plus and Advanced) let you make changes to current budgets or establish new ones. Reports that compare your actual income and spending to your projected budget may also be generated.

- You can set up, monitor, and manage your VAT using VAT. By informing you of the precise amount you owe and the due date, it helps you maintain tax compliance.
- Apps are where you can find other QuickBooks products and third-party apps.
- My accountant lets you interact and collaborate with your accountant from inside QuickBooks.

Personalize your view

You may change the navigation bar to hide pages you don't use or emphasize the websites you use most often to customize your menu to your needs. Navigate to ⬚ Menu options and then choose Customize to alter your view.

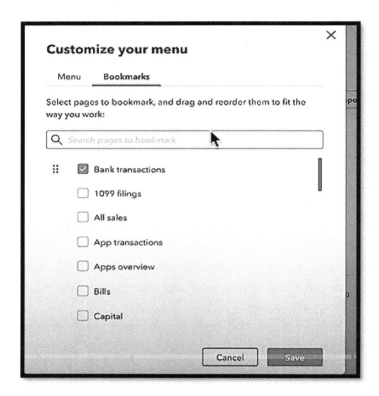

To reorganize, hide, or reveal your bookmarks or pages, just follow the instructions. Click the edit icon next to the menu choices to show, hide, or bookmark a page.

Save a page to your bookmarks

- Select Edit ✎ next to Bookmarks.

- Under Bookmarks, choose the pages you want to see.
- Pick, reorder, and drag your bookmarks into the proper order to reorganize them.
- Choose "Save."

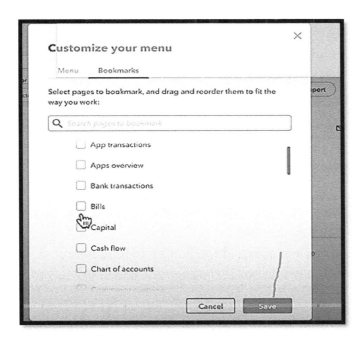

Use the procedures listed below to get a bookmark deleted:

- Click Edit ✎ next to Bookmarks.
- To delete a page from your bookmarks, uncheck the box next to it.
- Choose "Save."

Show or hide a page

- Select Edit next to Menu.
- Select the pages you need and uncheck the ones you don't.
- The pages you uncheck will be available under More.
- Select Reorder and drag the items to the correct order to reorganize your menu.
- Choose "Save."

It's easy to use keyboard shortcuts to expedite QuickBooks Online navigation. The following browsers are compatible with these shortcuts: Internet Explorer, Firefox, and Chrome are among the available browsers (unless otherwise noted). The quick reference guide is available in QuickBooks Online. Press Control + Option (Alt) +? (Mac) to bring up this screen.

Some of the keyboard shortcuts available in QuickBooks Online are listed below:

- How to get a second window to open

> o For Internet Explorer, use Ctrl + N. (Note that you will be signed in to the same company on both windows.)
> o For Firefox, use Ctrl + N. (Note: You will remain signed in to the first window but not in the second. The second window will enable you to log in to the current company so that you can operate from both displays.
> o For Chrome, use Ctrl + N. (Note: If you navigate to QuickBooks Online from that window, you will be logged in to the existing firm.)

- How to search a window for text

> o CTRL + F (works in Internet Explorer, Firefox, Chrome, and Internet Explorer) will open a pop-up search window.
> o Firefox displays a Find toolbar at the bottom of the screen.
> o Chrome displays a search box at the top right side of the screen.

- How dates are inserted

- o Next day + (plus key)
- o Previous day - (minus key)
- o Today T
- o First day of the Week W
- o Last day of the week K
- o First day of the Month M
- o Last day of the month H
- o First day of the Year Y
- o Last day of the year R
- o To launch the pop-up calendar icon located to the right of a date field, press the Alt+down arrow.

⊥ How to determine the rates and amounts

- o In any Amount or Rate field, put a calculation. When you press Tab, QuickBooks Online computes the result.
- o Add 1256.94 + 356.50 and subtract 48.95 -15.
- o Multiply 108*1.085.
- o Divide 89.95/.33.
- o Group () 13.95 + (25.95 *.75)

⊥ How to navigate most forms' fields

- o Press the Tab key to move forward.
- o To go back, use Shift+Tab.
- o To check a checkbox field, press the spacebar.

⊥ The process of choosing things from dropdown menus

- o Press Tab until you've reached the field.
- o To open the list, press Alt + Down Arrow.
- o To navigate the list, use the up and down arrows.
- o Tap the Tab icon to select the desired item and proceed to the next field.
- o If you don't want to open the entire list, but simply want to browse through the records in the text box, use Ctrl + down or Ctrl + up arrows.

+ How to choose things from a list with sub-items

> o Enter the first few letters of the parent item till it is selected.
>   ■ To access the list of sub-items, enter **the first few letters of the sub-item till it is chosen.**
>   ■ To open the list of sub-items, click the **Alt + down arrow, and then scroll through them by pressing the down arrow or up arrow.**
> o **Tap the Tab icon to choose the desired item and proceed to the next field.**

+ How forms are stored

> o Instead of hitting **Save, press Alt + S when in any form.**
> o In Firefox and Chrome, you must press Alt + Shift + S. For Mac users, it's Option + Control + S.

+ How to reply to messages

> o Press down **the Alt key.** If the button names contain underlined letters, you can choose the desired button by holding down the Alt key and typing the letter.

+ How to save or amend a selected transaction

> o To save, press **Alt+S. Alt + Shift + S (Firefox and Chrome).**
> o To modify a saved transaction, press **Alt + E.** This launches the transaction form.

+ How to navigate between transactions in the register while selecting the date field

> o To pick **the transaction shown above, press the up arrow.**
> o Press the **down arrow to pick the transaction listed below.**

+ Methods for modifying print alignment

> o Choose the **Vertical or Horizontal field,** then press "+" to increase the number or "-" to decrease it.
> o You must press **the keys on the numeric keypad.**

+ How an account register's transaction type may be selected

> o Press **Shift + Tab** in a new yellow transaction row to pick the transaction type field.
> o To open the list, press **Alt + Down Arrow.**
> o To move through the list, press the up or down arrows, or write the initial letter of the desired transaction type. If two transaction types start with the same letter, type it twice to choose the second one. For example, to pick **Check, input C** once, and then select **Cash Purchase.**
> o Press the **Tab icon** to pick the transaction type and proceed to the next field. Once you're comfortable with the available transaction kinds, you may go to the field and type the initial letter without accessing the list.

+ How to navigate through diary entries

> o In the Journal Entry screen, use the up arrow to move to the distribution line above, and the down arrow to move to the one below.

+ **How payroll is handled:** To start payroll, press CTRL + ALT + U after entering into QuickBooks Online or QuickBooks Payroll. (Mac: Control + Option + U)
   - ➤ This shortcut allows you to choose a pay plan for this payroll for a variety of pay schedules.
   - ➤ This provides a page where you may review employee pay information prior to processing payroll if you only have one pay schedule.

Creating a Business Profile

Investors and other stakeholders may learn more about a company's value, purpose, objectives, and performance by reading its profile. You can create a corporate profile that draws readers in and improves a firm's reputation by knowing what to include. A company profile may be made by the owner of a small business. On the other hand, larger companies may assign this duty to an employee.

The following are some uses for company profiles:
   + **Funding:** Prospective investors may use company profiles to get the information they need to decide whether to invest in a business.
   + **Branding:** A corporate profile may be used to tell visitors to your website and social media accounts about the origins, beliefs, and purpose of your business.
   + **Recruitment:** You may advertise your company to prospective workers and emphasize what makes it unique by creating a corporate profile, which is comparable to a corporate page on Indeed.

Corporate profiles are not required to have a certain length. While some profiles are 10 pages or more, others are as short as two pages. A number of variables, such as the size, age, and target audience of the business, might affect its duration. This section will teach you how to create your company profile, which involves controlling user roles and permissions, as well as providing corporate information and preferences.

Entering corporate preferences and business information

You may see and modify your company's name, address, phone number, and Employer Identification Number (EIN) under the Company page. Additionally, you may alter your Intuit marketing choices.

Modify or add your company's information

Make sure your company's information is current so that clients can locate and get in touch with you. Verify your company information again since QuickBooks contains features that depend on it. Note: In some situations, adding a different business could be a better option than altering your company details. For taxation reasons, this keeps your books distinct. It's generally best to file using a different EIN.

- Select Account and Settings by clicking on the Settings gear icon.

YOUR COMPANY	LISTS	TOOLS	PROFILE
Account and settings	All lists	Order cheques	Feedback
Manage users	Products and services	Import data	Privacy
Custom form styles	Recurring transactions	Import outside data	Switch company
Chart of accounts	Attachments	Export data	
Payroll settings	Custom fields	Reconcile	
QuickBooks labs	Tags	Budgeting	
Additional info		Audit log	
		SmartLook	

- To make changes to a section, choose Company first, then Edit✎. Take note: Update your business information in your payment and payroll accounts first if you get an error of -7000 or if you are unable to change the company name, legal name, or EIN.
- Choose "Save" and then "Done."

Change the name of your business

- Select Accounts and Settings after navigating to Settings ⬚ .
- Choose business and then ✎ to change the business name.
- In the "Company name" field, enter the new name.
  - ➢ Enter your legal name in the Legal name form if the company's legal name is different from the one you submitted.
  - ➢ If not, tick the box next to "Same as Company Name."
- Type or modify your Business Number (BN) in the designated field.
- Choose "Save" and then "Done."

Update your contact details

- Select Accounts and Settings after navigating to Settings ⬚ .
- To modify contact details, choose Company and then ✎.
- Provide a business email address so that QuickBooks may get in touch with you.
- Select the "same as corporate email" option in the customer-facing email section if you use the same email address for all of your customers.
- Type the business phone number that shows up on your sales documents.
- Enter your company's website URL as it appears on your sales forms in the Website box.
- Choose "Save" and then "Done."

Make sure your corporate addresses are up to current

- You may provide a maximum of three distinct addresses for your business:
- **Company address:** Your business's actual address.
- The address you use to interact with your consumers is known as the customer-facing address.
- **Legal address:** The address where tax returns are filed.
- **To change any of the company's addresses, adhere to the guidelines listed below;**
  - ➢ Select Accounts and Settings after navigating to Settings ⬚ .
  - ➢ To change the address, choose Company and then ✎.
  - ➢ Enter the main address for your business in the Company address field.

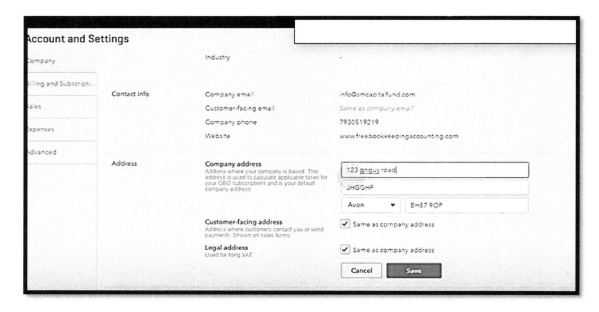

+ **In the address box that faces customers:**
  ➢ Provide a contact or payment address that your clients may utilize to get in touch with you.
  ➢ Check the "same as company address" box if the address matches the one you supplied.
+ **In the field for the legal address:**
  ➢ Enter the legal address you use to submit your firm's taxes.
  ➢ Alternatively, select the box labeled "same as company address" if the address you supplied is the same.
+ **Choose "Save" and then "Done."**

Update your selections for Intuit's promotional offerings

+ In the Communications with Intuit section, choose Company and then click the Marketing Preferences option.
+ Go to Settings ☐ and select Accounts and Settings.
+ Go to the Intuit Account Manager page and add or modify the information to customize your goods.
+ Save the modifications once you're done.

Usage: You may see the number of billable users, accounts, and tag groups in your company by selecting the Usage tab.

Sales: You may create payment terms, personalize your sales forms, and control what data shows up on client forms by going to the Sales page. You may also activate features like automatic reminders and progress invoicing here.

Progress Invoicing: With progress invoicing, you may split an estimate into as many bills as needed. Instead of anticipating full payment at the beginning of a work, you might bill clients for partial payments. As you complete the job, add items from the original estimate to progress invoices. This keeps project payments organized and connected from start to finish. **The steps to activate progress invoicing are as follows:**

+ Click the Settings gear icon to choose Account and Settings.

+ Navigate the sales tab

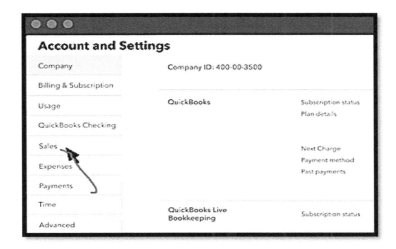

✦ In the Progress Invoicing area, choose Edit.

✦ Turn on the setting that lets you use a single estimate to generate many partial invoices.

✦ Select Update from the "Update your invoice template" popup.
✦ Press Save, then Finish.

Use the following procedures to create a progress invoice template: If you activate this feature, QuickBooks creates a default progress invoicing template automatically. Use the given Airy new style template each time you create a progress invoice. **To create a new template, follow these steps:**

✦ In order to generate a fresh invoice template, choose the New

+ Next, choose Invoice.

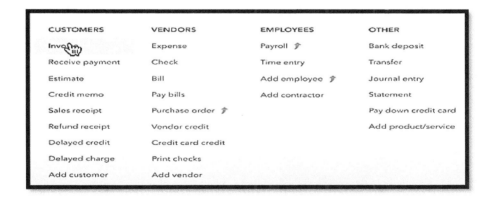

Otherwise, to update one of your existing templates, find the template and choose Edit.

+ Give the template a distinctive and snappy name, like "Progress invoice template."

+ From the Design menu, choose Alter the template or Start using a template. Select the updated Airy template. This template is the only one that works with progress invoices.

+ If you're not sure, either print it out or choose Adjust Print Settings. Make sure you have not chosen the "Fit printed form with pay stub in window envelope" option.

+ Select the Content tab.

+ Choose Edit ✏ in the forms table section (the second one that has Activity, Rate, and Amount). Select the link that says "Show more activity options." Select the

42

Show progress on line items checkbox to show item information on the progress invoice.

⨪ Choose Edit ✎ in the bottom of the form (the third section with Balance Due and Total). Choose the estimated summary if you want the invoice to display the estimated amount, the total of the individual progress invoices, and the total amount invoiced so far.

⨪ Press "Done." You'll be sent back to the Custom Form Styles page.

⨪ If you send out a lot of progress invoices, it is recommended that you adopt this as your new template for all invoices. **In order to make the freshly created template your default template:**

➢ For those who haven't previously, go back to Custom form styles.

➢ Next to the template in the Action column, choose the dropdown menu (▼). Then choose Set as default.

➢ To validate your choices, click on the Change template.

Design Note: You may create a second default template for normal invoices if you merely desire to utilize this template for a limited number of progress invoices. You may then use the same invoice template the next time you generate a new invoice by selecting Customize directly on the invoice form.

Making an estimate

⨪ After selecting + New

+ Choose Estimate.

+ Select your customer.

+ Fill in the rest of the estimate. Select whether to save and send, save and close, or save and new.
+ Please be aware that the totals in the remaining column of your estimate do not include shipping, discount, or sales tax.

Using the estimate to generate a progress invoice

+ Go to Sales, and then choose "All sales."

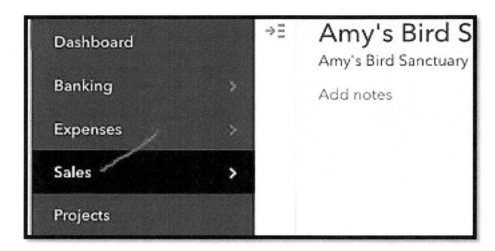

+ Find the estimate on the list.
+ After opening the estimate, choose "Create invoice" from the dropdown menu.

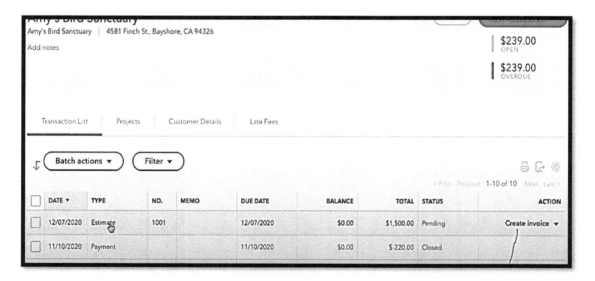

+ Click Create Invoice after the amount to be invoiced has been decided. You may choose to charge a percentage or a set amount. If you choose Custom amount for each line, enter a different amount for each item on the invoice.

- Fill out the rest of the invoice.
- Select whether to save and close, save and share links, or save and new.

Attach a new invoice to an estimate

- Select Add New, followed by Invoice.
- Select your customer from the drop-down menu. If the customer has an open estimate, QuickBooks will display the Add to Invoice sidebar.
- After finding the estimate in the sidebar, choose Add.
- Once the amount to be invoiced has been determined, choose Copy to invoice.
- Fill out the rest of the invoice.
- Select whether to save and close, save and share links, or save and new.

Your initial estimate won't change if you create a progress invoice. QuickBooks keeps track of both.

About Expenses

You may change the email messages that go with purchase orders and enable billable costs and buy orders on the expenses page.

The Billable expenses

To activate billable costs, do the actions listed below:
- To input billable charges, activate billable expenditure monitoring.
- After selecting Settings [], choose Account and Settings.

➕ Go to the section on expenses.

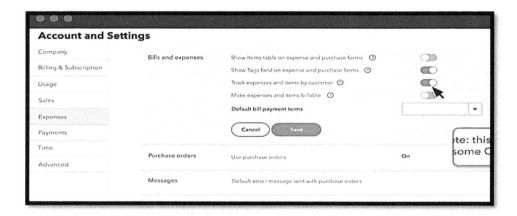

➕ From the Bills and Expenses section, choose Edit ✿.
➕ **Turn on the following:**
  ➢ Show the items table on the forms for purchases and expenses.
  ➢ Monitor items and expenses by client.
  ➢ Charge for products and costs.
➕ After completing the aforementioned, you have the option to set up the following:
  ➢ Markup rate and billable expenditure monitoring.
➕ Payment conditions for bills
➕ Select Save.

Add a billable expenditure

The methods for billing a consumer for expenditure are listed below.

➕ Select + New.

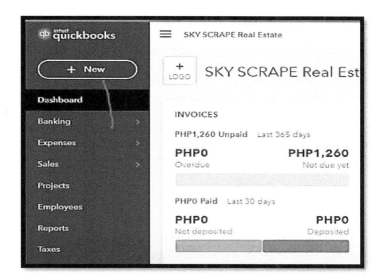

+ You may create a check, bill, or expenditure to initiate a transaction.

+ Choose the person who will be paid.
+ From the Category column, choose the spending account for the transaction.
+ Check the Billable box once the expenditure description and amount have been entered.
+ From the list in the client column, choose the customer you want to charge for this expenditure.
+ Details are optional. After entering or confirming the markup percentage, pick a tax agency or check the Tax option if you want to charge tax.
+ Select "Save and Close."

Billable expenditure inclusion in invoices

To get your money back, attach the chargeable expenditure to your customer's invoice.

- Select + New.
- Select the invoice.
- From the client dropdown menu, select the customer for whom you generated a chargeable expenditure. This causes the Add to Invoice box to open.
- Decide whether you want to charge your customer for any chargeable expenditures.
- Select "Save and Close."

Payments

You may link an existing QuickBooks Payments account to QuickBooks Online or create online payments using the Payments option. Once linked, you may instruct QuickBooks on where to keep deposits and modify merchant and company owner data. You must first understand how to get QuickBooks Payments (Merchant Services) in order to handle client payments in QuickBooks. You can manage your accounts and make payments in most QuickBooks products using QuickBooks Payments. QuickBooks Payments allows you to accept credit card payments and will categorize each transaction on your chart of accounts.

Register with QuickBooks Online

In order to receive payments, you must first register using QuickBooks Online. QuickBooks Payments will be available to a large number of customers.

The Payments registration window is divided into three sections:

- Please fill out the "About your business" section with details about your company. When you're done, choose Save to continue.
- Make changes to the "About You" portion of the form, then click "Save and continue."
- Under the "Your Deposit Account" section, choose a different bank account to receive payments from your clients. Click Add and search for your bank if you choose a different bank account. Click Connect after your bank's login information has been entered.
- After finishing each section, click Review and exit.

You will get an email about your registration in a few business days. If approved, you may place orders for things like a mobile card reader right from the email.

About Subscription & Billing

You may recover your business ID, change your payment method, upgrade or decrease your QuickBooks Online membership, and even resubscribe on the Billing & membership page.

View the details of your subscription

+ Sign in as the main administrator in QuickBooks Online.
+ Go to Settings ⬚ and choose Billing and Subscriptions.

+ Examine each section's content
+ Go to the QuickBooks Online tile and choose "Access Payment History" to see your payment history. The invoices from the last six months are shown in your billing history.

Modify or update your mode of payment

+ Sign in to QuickBooks Online as the main administrator.
+ To access Billing and Subscriptions, go to Settings ⬚.
+ Next to your payment method, click Edit.
+ Update your credit card details.
+ Check the address on the credit card. It must match the one that appears on your credit card statements.
+ After you're done, choose Confirm card or Save card.

Footnote: If QuickBooks Online and Payroll are combined, this also changes the credit card details linked to your payroll subscription. If you have many Intuit subscriptions, you may establish and retrieve payment methods for each one using Intuit Payment Wallet.

Access your payment history

- Log in as the primary administrator.
- After selecting Settings ⬚, choose Billing and Subscriptions.
- **The QuickBooks Online tile offers the option to see payment history.**
  - ➢ The billing history will be shown chronologically, starting with the most recent bill.
  - ➢ Billing statements are accessible the day after the billing date, but not on the same day.
  - ➢ If you signed in as an accountant, you will not be able to obtain the billing Portable Document Format (PDF) file for a customer who pays for their membership.

Modify your billing schedule

Learn how to change your QuickBooks Online subscription's billing cycle. QuickBooks Online offers monthly and yearly price choices for Essentials, EasyStart, Plus, and Advanced. When you're ready, follow these steps to modify your payment plan. After completing the steps below, you will get an email with the details of your new plan. **"If you have a QuickBooks Online subscription, do the following tasks:**
- Sign in to QuickBooks Online as the main administrator.
- After selecting Settings ⬚, choose Billing and Subscriptions.

- Decide whether to use monthly billing or yearly billing.
- Select Switch, and then, all right, I understand.
- **If there is a free trial period for your QuickBooks package, do the following:**
  - ➢ Log in to access your QuickBooks Online account.
  - ➢ Press the Subscribe button. Complete all the required fields.
  - ➢ Select either the monthly or annual billing option from the subscription summary.
  - ➢ Select "Submit," and then "Okay, I understand."

The time tab

On the Time tab, you may choose the start day of the workweek, record the services your team rendered to a client, and indicate whether or not you want staff and suppliers to be able to see the amount you charge customers for their labor.

The Advanced

You may click the extra tab in QuickBooks to activate more options. By default, not all are activated. To monitor goods and services in a certain manner, for instance, you might activate categories. The beginning and end of your company's fiscal year are also specified here. You may also activate this feature here if your company handles several currencies. What your clients see on sales forms and invoices depends on your account settings. Additionally, it is your internal data that is stored with Intuit. You may always make changes in the settings if necessary.

Concerning Multicurrency

Using multicurrency allows you to make and receive payments in foreign currencies from clients, suppliers, or bank accounts that do not use your local currency. When you create transactions in multiple currencies, QuickBooks handles all currency conversions once it is enabled. **Note:** A single currency may be given to most account types, including suppliers, customers, and accounts in the chart of accounts (including bank and credit card accounts or accounts receivable). For each currency you use in transactions, you have to open a new account.

Turn Multicurrency on

The currency that your business uses for transactions is usually the home currency, depending on where it is based. Your income and spending accounts are always in your local currency. When you initially set up QuickBooks, it automatically decides your native currency. **If required, you may change your local currency:**
   + Click the Settings gear icon to choose Account & Settings, and then
   + Select Advanced.

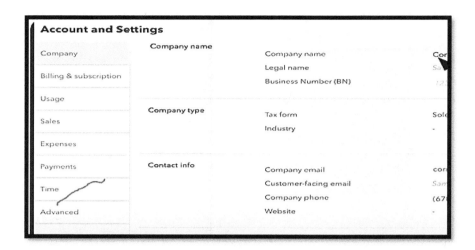

+ In the Currency section, choose Edit ✓.

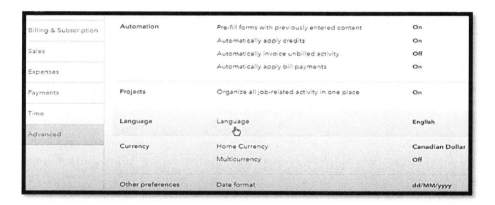

+ From the Home Currency ▼menu, choose your currency.
+ Turn on the Multicurrency option and accept that this is a permanent configuration.
+ Press Save, then Finish.

What happens when Multicurrency is activated?

+ Your chart of accounts shows account balances in the specified currencies in addition to a currency column that indicates the currency of each account.
+ Instead of creating distinct reports for every currency, QuickBooks creates financial reports in your native currency. These include profits or losses associated with currency rates.
+ Certain product features may not operate once this feature is engaged.

Include currencies

+ To access the Settings gear icon, navigate.
+ Decide which currencies to use. Note: This option is available after multi-currency has been enabled.
+ Then choose "Add currency."
+ Select the new currency from the Add Currency ▼dropdown menu.
+ Press Add.

Include an account that uses foreign currencies

Your native currency will be shown as the default for any existing accounts in the Currency column of the Chart of Accounts. **To open a foreign exchange account,**
+ Choose the Chart of Accounts option by navigating to the Settings gear icon.
+ Select New.

+ Select the appropriate Account Type and Detail Type.

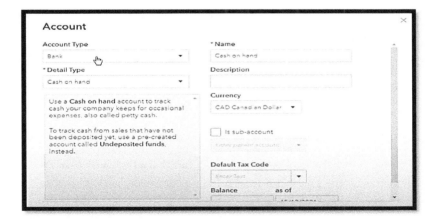

- Give the new account a name, enter any other information that is needed, and add a description if you'd like.
- Select the foreign currency to be linked to the account from the Currency ▼ dropdown menu.

- Enter the date and opening balance when you initially start recording business transactions. Enter the whole amount in your account that day.
- Press "Save" and "Close."

Add foreign currency transactions

If you have banks linked to your QuickBooks Online account, you may enter transactions in foreign currencies.
- Go to Transactions to see bank transactions.
- Click Add after opening the transaction information from the For Review page.
- In the currency columns, enter the foreign amount or the exchange rate that your bank provides.

QuickBooks Online calculates the total and displays the transaction in the Bank Detail or Description sections just as your bank did on your account, including the amount and currency. Note: You may deposit foreign currency into a linked foreign bank account if you have QuickBooks Payments enabled, but you cannot bill a foreign client in a foreign currency.

Make a deposit at a bank using a different currency

Multicurrency allows you to deposit funds in a different currency at a bank.
- Pay the invoice by depositing it into a bank account in the same currency.
- Select + New.
- Select Transfer.

- Choose accounts for each field.
  - ➤ Transfer Money from The account where the money is taken out.
  - ➤ Money Transfer To The account that receives the money.
  - ➤ **Currency:** The currency you choose determines the amount that is entered in the Transfer Amount section. You also need to input the currency rate if you haven't previously.
  - ➤ For example, you may choose US dollars as the currency and enter $5.00 in the Transfer Amount field. Five US dollars is the amount that QuickBooks transfers.
  - ➤ The amount you will transfer to the account is known as the "Amount to Be Transferred." This sum's total value is not absolute since it depends on the currency and exchange rate.
- Enter the invoice's payment amount in the Transfer Amount area.
- Click Save and Close after the invoice date has been entered.

Use a different currency for paying staff

Employers may need to pay workers in a different currency in this era of remote employment. More information on how to do this is provided in the stages that follow. **Initially, you will need to utilize your employee information to establish a supplier. To do this, take the actions listed below:**
- After expenses, navigate to suppliers.
- After selecting "New supplier," fill in the fields with the personnel details.
- Choose a currency from the Currency ▼ menu.

- After adding a currency to their display name, choose Save.

- After completing the aforementioned procedures, you may pay your employee by following the steps listed below:
  - Select + New.
  - Select the cost.
  - From the Payee dropdown menu, choose the supplier you established using your employee's information.
  - From the Category ▼ menu, choose the account you use to monitor your payroll expenses, then
  - Click Save.

Linking Credit Cards and Bank Accounts

By connecting your bank or credit card account to QuickBooks Online, you may speed up your accounting process and save a lot of time. You won't have to manually input transactions as a result. Before you start, make sure you have the following in place: Check to see whether your bank supports Open Banking connections. If you can't find your bank, you may manually add transactions in its stead. If you have a foreign currency account, here's how to open one.

- To connect accounts for cash on hand, follow these steps.
- Connecting bank accounts to enable smooth transactions

Connect your bank account or credit card to save inputting your transactions by hand. You may connect several businesses and personal bank accounts in QuickBooks to keep up-to-date corporate information. You may connect your American Express Business account to your QuickBooks Online account.

This is done in a number of phases.

- After selecting Transactions, choose Bank transactions.
- Select "Link Account."
- Enter your bank's name or URL in the search window, and then choose the bank.

Footnote: If you can't find your bank, you may manually submit transactions.

- Click Proceed after entering your login credentials in the Password and Login fields.
- Choose the date and the account you want to connect to from the dropdown menu to extract transactions. Then choose that option. Take note: Some banks allow you to see transactions for the last ninety days. Some are able to go back up to 24 months.
- Click Next after selecting your account type from the Account type ▼menu. **Note:** Choose the account type in QuickBooks based on your chart of accounts. If the correct account type is not shown, choose +Add new.

+ To open a new bank account, do the following:

> Select Bank from the Account Type dropdown option.

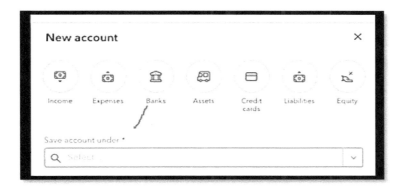

> Under Detail Type, choose either checking or savings.

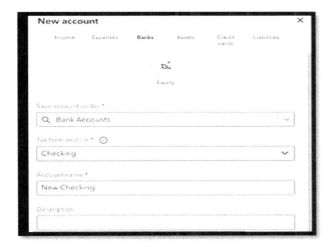

> Once the account has been named, choose Save and Close.

+ For brand-new credit card accounts,

> Choose Credit Card from the Account Type dropdown option.

➢ Once the account has been named, choose Save and Close.

✦ After mapping the bank account in the Existing Accounts ▼menu, choose Next.

✦ Select Connect, then select Done. **Note:** You may change the account name in the New Account Name section or later.

✦ To link your bank account to your chart accounts, follow the instructions below.

➢ Select the Chart of Accounts by navigating to the Settings gear icon.

➢ In the Action column, choose the View Register ▼option.

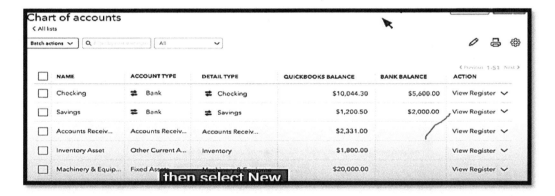

➢ Next, choose Connect Bank.

✦ Enter your bank's name or URL in the search window, and then choose the bank. Note: If you can't find your bank, you may manually submit transactions.

✦ Click Proceed after entering your login credentials in the Password and Login fields.

✦ Choose the date and the account you want to connect to from the dropdown menu to extract transactions. Then choose that option. Note: Some banks allow you to see transactions for the last ninety days. Some are able to go back up to 24 months.

+ Click Next after selecting your account type from the Account type ▼menu.

Keep in mind: Choose the account type in QuickBooks based on your chart of accounts. If the correct account type is not shown, choose +Add new.

    + **To open a new bank account, do the following:**
        ➢ From the Account Type ▼dropdown menu, choose Bank.
        ➢ After naming the account, choose Save and Close.
        ➢ Under Detail Type, select either checking or savings.
    + **For brand-new credit card accounts,**
        ➢ Choose Credit Card from the Account Type dropdown option.
        ➢ Once the account has been named, choose Save and Close.
    + After mapping the bank account in the Existing Accounts ▼ menu, choose Next.
    + Select Connect, then select Done. Note: You may change the account name in the New Account Name section or later.

To download your recent bank accounts promptly, refresh your bank feed by following these steps:
    + Go to Transactions, and then choose Bank transactions.
    + Select an update.

Account reconciliation and bank feed setup

Making bank account reconciliations

Just like you would with a checkbook balance, you should verify that your QuickBooks accounts match your bank and credit card payments. This process is known as reconciling. You will need to compare each transaction on your bank statement with the ones that QuickBooks has entered. If everything matches, you may be certain that your accounts are balanced and correct. A regular reconciliation of your bank, savings, and credit card accounts is advised. Here's how to get started.

Examine your starting balance

When you are initially reconciling an account, look at the opening balance. It must match the amount on the day you choose to start recording transactions from your real bank account in QuickBooks. Advice: You may save a step by connecting your bank and credit cards to online banking, which will retrieve transactions instantly and input the starting balance for you. Note: The options to add a service fee and interest earned are only accessible if the bank account isn't connected to internet banking.

Start the process of reconciliation

As soon as you get your monthly credit card or bank statement, you may start reconciling. **Work on one statement at a time, starting with the oldest, when reconciling data from many months:**
- If your accounts are connected to Internet banking, make sure the transactions you downloaded match and belong to the right categories.
- Select Reconcile after navigating to the gear-shaped Settings icon.

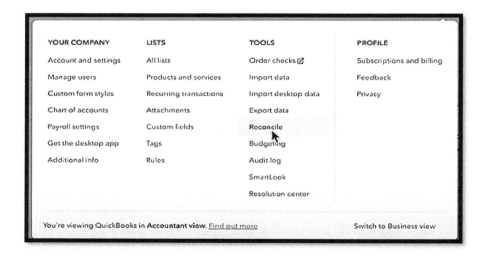

- If this is your first time reconciling, choose Get Started.
- From the Account dropdown menu, choose the account you want to reconcile.

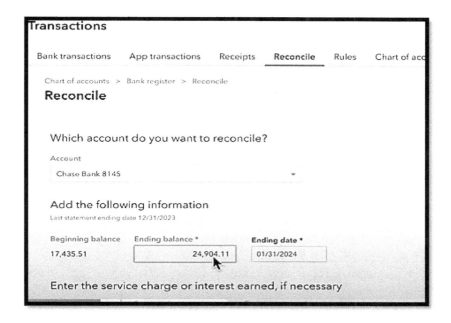

Make sure it matches the one on your statement. Crucial: Select If you get a notice about a previous reconciliation, we can assist you in resolving it. You have to correct something before you start.

- Analyze the initial balance. Make sure the beginning balance in QuickBooks and on your statement match.
- Enter the closing date and ending balance on your statement. The final balance is often referred to by banks as the "new balance" or the "closing balance."
- If you detect it, look at the last statement's expiration date. Your most recent reconciliation comes to an end now. Your current bank statement should start the next day.
- Select Start Reconciliation when you're ready to get started.

Check your statement against QuickBooks

At this stage, just match the transactions in QuickBooks with those on your statement. Review each one in isolation. The challenging aspect is making sure you have the right dates and payments in QuickBooks so you know everything matches. **Depending on the kind of account you're reconciling, you should follow this section:**

Balancing accounts linked to internet banking

- Reconciling should be easy since your bank gives you all the transaction data. In some cases, your accounts could already be balanced.

- First, look at the first transaction on your statement.
- Find the same transaction in the Reconciliation box of QuickBooks.
- Analyze how the two transactions vary from one another. If they match, mark the amount in QuickBooks using a checkbox. It is currently regarded as settled. To speed up the procedure, transactions that you added or matched from online banking have already been selected for you.
- If you see a transaction in QuickBooks but it doesn't appear on your statement, don't mark it.
- Check each transaction on your statement against the information in QuickBooks.

Hint: If you are certain that you have discovered a match but there is a little problem that has to be resolved, such as the payee, don't worry. In QuickBooks, choose the transaction to enlarge the display. Then choose Edit. Modify the specifics to support your claim.

- The ultimate discrepancy between your statement and QuickBooks should be zero dollars. Click Finish immediately if so.

Account reconciliation for those connected to internet banking

Can't get into your online banking account? Not a problem. What you ought to do is this:
- First, look at the first transaction on your statement.
- Find the same transaction in the QuickBooks Reconciliation box.
- Look at how the two transactions vary. If they match, mark the amount in QuickBooks using a checkbox. It is currently regarded as settled.
- If you see a transaction in QuickBooks but it doesn't appear on your statement, don't mark it.
- Check each transaction on your statement against the information in QuickBooks.
- Advice: If you are certain that you have discovered a match but there is a little problem that has to be resolved, such as the payee, don't worry. In QuickBooks, choose the transaction to enlarge the display. Then choose Edit. Modify the specifics to support your claim.
- The ultimate discrepancy between your statement and QuickBooks should be zero dollars. Click Finish immediately if so.

Configuring bank feeds

Using Bank Feeds, you may connect your credit card and bank accounts to QuickBooks Desktop's online banking. By uploading your bank transactions, you may avoid manually documenting them. There are two ways to register for an account. There are two ways to connect: Web Connect and Direct Connect. How you connect will depend on what your bank has to offer. There are two ways to register for an account. There are two ways to connect: Web Connect and Direct Connect. How you connect will depend on what your bank has to offer. You will need the password or PIN for your bank in order to use this method. After the account is set up, you may download your electronic statements to your bank feeds. When you download transactions for the first time, QuickBooks automatically establishes a Bank Feeds account. Before moving further, find out from your bank whether the service is free or has a fee. Your bank provides your Customer ID and password (sometimes known as a PIN) for online banking setup.

You may also need to have these:

- **Account Number:** Your FI provides this number to your account when it is formed. It is shown on your bank statements. If you can't find it, get in touch with your FI.

- **Routing Number:** FIs are assigned a nine-digit routing number. It typically appears on an account check. If you can't find it, get in touch with your FI.

- **Account type:** You should understand how your financial institution functions rather than how QuickBooks classifies your account.
  - From Banking, go to Bank Feeds.
  - Choose Set up Bank Feeds for an account.
  - In the area labeled "Enter the name of your bank," type in and choose your bank.

- If this is your first time enrolling, choose the link to the Enrollment Site. It may be necessary for you to submit an application via Direct Connect. If your bank needs to approve your application, contact them. Ask if you need any special login information. **After enrolling, complete the following tasks:**
  - Click "Continue."
  - To access online banking, enter your user ID and password.
  - Click Connect to connect your QuickBooks to your bank's server.
  - To connect your QuickBooks account to a bank account, choose one.
  - Choose Finish after the connection is complete.

Use Web Connect (.QBO) files to connect

If your bank does not permit direct connection, you may get a file (.QBO) that contains the transactions of your business from your credit card or bank. You next import the file into QuickBooks to add those transactions to your accounts.

If your bank offers Web Connect:

- Click Import Web Connect Files after selecting Bank Feeds from Banking.
- Click Open after selecting the.QBO file you saved.
- **Upon being asked to choose a bank account:**
  - Use the account that QuickBooks has already set up if it is the account into which you are importing transactions.

> ➤ Make a new account in QuickBooks if the one you are importing transactions into isn't already there.
- Click "Continue." When the data has been successfully read into QuickBooks, a dialog box will show up. Press OK.
- To review the transactions you submitted, go to the Bank Feeds Center.

Modify bank feed settings for credit card or bank accounts

You may change your bank account login information and other settings using QuickBooks Desktop. Simply disable your bank feeds if you want to make any changes. Then set up your bank feeds again.
- Disconnect the bank feeds associated with your account.
- Make the required modifications.
- Set up the bank feeds for your account.

Practice Exercises

- Establish and maintain your account.
- Which subscription options are available in QuickBooks Online?
- To increase productivity, personalize your office.
- Learn more about how to use shortcuts and navigation menus.
- Modify your account's billing and subscription options, sales, costs, and payments.
- Make bank account reconciliations

CHAPTER THREE
FINANCIAL MANAGEMENT USING ONLINE QUICKBOOKS

Effective financial management is essential to a company's success. QuickBooks Online offers a plethora of features and tools to help companies better manage their finances. QuickBooks Online provides a number of functions, including budgeting, cash flow management, compliance, and financial reporting, to streamline financial operations and increase accuracy so you can make well-informed choices. As a result, businesses may focus on growth and strategic objectives, secure in the knowledge that their financial administration is in capable hands.

Documenting and Monitoring Earnings

QuickBooks Online makes it easy to keep track of company expenses in addition to tracking sales. Entering your income and costs gives you a more complete picture of your business's profits. If you have already paid for a business cost, enter it here. However, if you plan to pay for the spending later, include it as a bill. QuickBooks is instructed on how to record each transaction by these specific transaction types. Here's how to record and monitor costs in QuickBooks.

Documenting an Expense

Use these procedures if you need to record a business cost in QuickBooks that you have previously paid for:

+ Select + New. Then choose Expense.

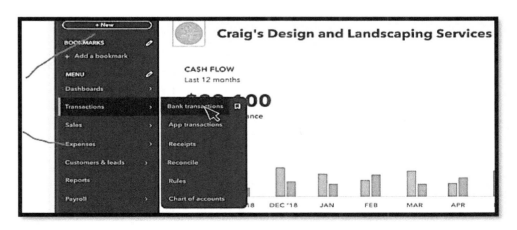

⁜ In the Payee section, choose the vendor.

Tips: Leave this box empty if the transaction covers more than one petty cash cost.

⁜ In the Payment Account section, choose the account you used to pay for the item.

⁜ In the Payment date field, enter the date of the cost.

⁜ Select the method of payment that you used to pay for it.

⁜ To get comprehensive tracking, input a permit or reference number. This is something you can decide not to do.

⁜ Enter the correct label in the Tags section to classify your cash.

⁜ Next, fill in the Category details box with the spending information. Next, choose from the Category menu whatever expense account you use to monitor expenditure transactions.

⁜ Lastly, include a description. Enter certain goods and services in the Item Details area to break down the cost by item. Put in the tax and amount.

⁜ Lastly, put the customer's name in the Customer field and select the Billable option if you want to charge them for the expenditure.

⁜ After you've finished the aforementioned, choose Save and close.

Making sales receipts and invoices

About Invoices

Sales transactions from customers that pay nothing or only a fraction of the entire amount owed at the time of sale are recorded on the invoice. Invoices may be used to manage your accounts receivable. Depending on the specifics of your customer transaction, QuickBooks Desktop offers many methods to create an invoice.

To build an invoice from scratch, follow these steps:

If your business does not need the creation of estimates or sales orders, your A/R process starts with the creation of the invoice.

- From the Customers menu or the Home screen, choose Create Invoices.

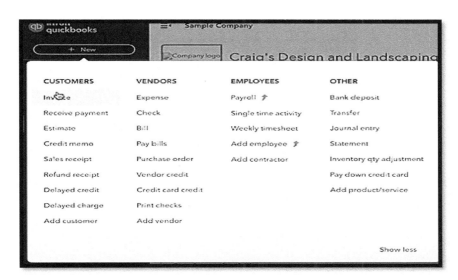

- From the Customer: task drop-down menu, choose a customer or customer task.

If the customer or job isn't in the list yet, you may choose Add New.

- At the top of the form, provide the required information, including the Terms, Date Invoice #, and Bill to/sold to.
- Pick one or more things from the detail section. Note: Depending on the description and unit cost selected during setup, the description and quantity are automatically supplied when you choose or add an item. This may be changed or removed when creating invoices.

- ⊹ (Optional) to be eligible for a discount, you have to make a discounted item.
  - ➤ From the Home screen, choose the Lists menu.
  - ➤ Select the list of items.
  - ➤ Anywhere you do a right-click, choose New.
  - ➤ Select Discount from the Type drop-down menu.

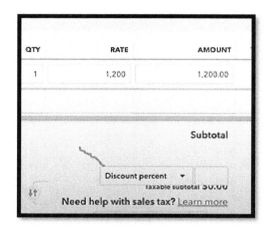

  - ➤ Include the name or number of the item along with a brief description.
  - ➤ In the Amount or % field, type the discount's amount or percentage. If your discount amounts differ, you may decide to put the discount amount directly on your sales forms and leave the Amount or % box blank.
  - ➤ Using the Account drop-down option, choose the revenue account you want to use to keep track of the discounts you provide to customers.
  - ➤ Select the appropriate tax code for the item.
  - ➤ Click "OK."
- ⊹ Select "Save and Close."

Prepare a sales order invoice

If you have created a sales order and completed it, you need to create an invoice. **There are two ways to do this:**
- ⊹ Select the "Create Invoice" button from the Sales Orders window, which is situated on the Sales Orders main tab.
- ⊹ When the option appears, choose Create invoice for all of the sales orders to include every item from the sales order in the invoice. Select Create Invoice for the selected items if you want to include only a subset of the items on the invoice.

+ Make the necessary changes to the invoice. Note: Fill in the To Invoice (Or Invoiced) column with the amount of each item in the list. If you do not want to invoice any of the items in the list, enter 0 (zero) as the quantity.
+ Press "Save & Close."

From the window for the invoice

+ From the QuickBooks Home page or the Customer menu, choose Create Invoices.
+ From the Customer: task drop-down menu, choose a customer or customer task.
+ The period for open sales orders begins.
+ Choose one or more sales orders that include the goods you want to charge for.
+ Make the necessary changes to the invoice. Note: Fill in the To Invoice (Or Invoiced) column with the amount of each item in the list. If you do not want to invoice any of the items in the list, enter 0 (zero) as the quantity.
+ Select "Save and Close."

Make an estimate-related invoice

If your client accepts your estimate and agrees to pay a set amount (rather than for real time and expenses), you may convert your estimate into an invoice in its entirety.

From the window for estimation;
+ Start the precise estimate.
+ Choose Create Invoice at the top of the Estimate form.
+ If you have progress invoicing enabled, you may get a popup asking what goods and quantities to include on the invoice. Please indicate what you would want to add as requested.
+ When the invoice shows up, make any required changes to the data.
+ Press "Save & Close."

From the window for the invoice

+ From the QuickBooks Home page or the Customer menu, choose Create Invoices.
+ From the Customer: task drop-down menu, choose a customer or customer task.
+ The range of estimations becomes accessible.
+ Decide which estimate you would want to see on the bill. Remember that with QuickBooks, you can only choose one estimate to invoice. Note: If you have progress invoicing enabled, you may get a popup requesting for details to be included on the invoice. You may just specify what should be included when asked.
+ When the invoice shows up, make any required changes to the data.
+ Press "Save & Close."

The Sales receipt

If your customer immediately pays for the products or services, create a sales receipt. Adding several sales receipts at once is possible with QuickBooks Online Advanced. To create both single and numerous sales receipts, follow the recommended steps outlined in this section.

Make a receipt for sales

Make your customer a sales receipt by hand in QuickBooks Online.

- Select Sales Receipt by clicking Add New.

- From the client ▼dropdown menu, choose a client.

If you haven't previously set up your client, note: Click + Add new.

⊹ Select the product or service you sold from the Choose a product/service ▼menu.

⊹ Details are optional. You may modify your line item's quantity or rate in the Qty and Rate field.

⊹ Click Save after filling out the remaining sections on the sales receipt.

Multiple sales receipts may be imported into QuickBooks Online Advanced using batch transactions and CSV import. You may enter many sales receipts at once more easily as a result. To submit more than one sales receipt, turn on the Show Product/Service column in the sales forms option. Because the *The Product/Service field won't seem to be missing, mapping QuickBooks data to your CSV file will flow more easily.

⊹ After choosing the Sales option, choose the Products and Services section.

⊹ If the choices are not selected, activate the Show Product/Service column on the sales form. Proceed to Step 2 if it is already switched on.

- ✚ After selecting Save, choose Done.

If you have several sales receipts, choose the Import via CSV option. This enables you to upload sales receipts automatically and promptly.

- ✚ Select Batch transactions by clicking Add New.
- ✚ From the Select Transaction Type ▼dropdown menu, pick sales receipts.
- ✚ Select "Import CSV."
- ✚ Take note: The Invoice Date column in the Batch transaction field may only include dates in the following formats: MM/DD/YYYY. Make sure you modify the cell content in the CSV file.
- ✚ Click Open after you've selected the CSV file you want to upload from Browse.(Details are optional.) To add all new customers to QuickBooks, check the corresponding box. This allows you to add customers who aren't listed in your QuickBooks account from your CSV file.
- ✚ Press Next.
- ✚ Make that the column headings in your CSV file match the appropriate QuickBooks fields.
- ✚ Press Next. Note: To find out what's generating the error, move your mouse over any red-highlighted fields. Follow the recommended steps to attempt to fix the issue.
- ✚ Select "Save."

Keeping track of payments and managing customer transactions

Maintaining structure and customer monitoring is essential as your business grows. By adding customer profiles to QuickBooks Online, you may include them in invoices or transactions. Here's how to add new customers and change your existing client list.

Bring on a new customer

Add your clients to the customer list in QuickBooks Online so you can monitor their upcoming transactions.

Here's the method:

- ✚ After visiting sales, choose your customers.
- ✚ Select the option "New customer."

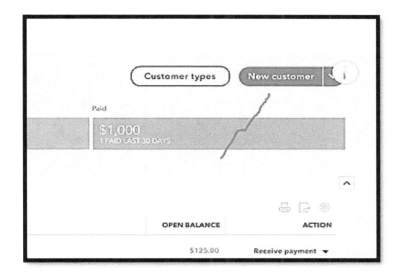

➕ In the Customer display name field, type the material you want the customer to see. (This field is required.) Next, review each area and add any more relevant customer information.

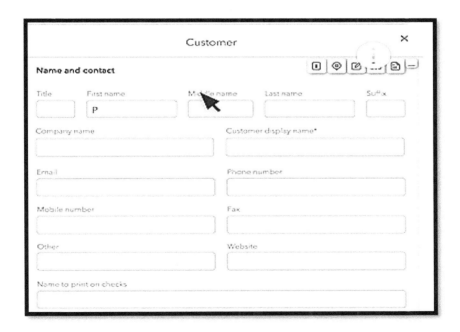

➕ If the client is exempt from paying taxes, tick the "This customer is tax exempt" box in the "Additional info" section. Next, choose the reason for their tax exemption from the drop-down option located under "Reason for exemption."

+ Click "Save."

A sub-customer Addition

You have the option to establish sub-customers under your top-level clients, often known as parent clients. If you want to keep an eye on certain customers who are also connected to a bigger business or organization, this is useful. You can have an unlimited number of sub-customers, but parent accounts can only have four tiers of sub-customers. If you haven't previously, add the parent customer as a new customer by following the previous steps. **Add each of the subsequent sub-customers after that:**

+ Go to Sales and choose Customers.
+ Select the option "New customer."
+ Enter the sub-customer's name and contact information.
+ Press the checkmark next to "Is a sub-customer." A parent customer dropdown menu will then show up as a result.
+ From the parent client's dropdown menu, choose the parent account.
+ Select the charge Parent checkbox if you want to charge the sub-customer in addition to the parent customer. Leave this unchecked if you want to bill the sub-customer directly.
+ Examine every section and provide any information you think the sub-customer needs to know.
+ Click on the Additional information section and check the box next to "There is no tax on this consumer" to see whether the sub-customer is exempt from paying taxes. Next, choose the justification for Exemption ▼dropdown menu to determine the customer's tax exemption justification.
+ Click "Save."

Handling Purchases and Expenses

QuickBooks Online makes it easy to keep track of company expenses in addition to tracking sales. Entering your income and costs gives you a more complete picture of your business's profits. If you plan to pay for it later, include the cost as a bill. Bills for several suppliers may be submitted concurrently or one at a time. If the business expenditure has already been covered, report the item as an expense instead. These specific transaction types provide QuickBooks instructions on how to input all of the information. Here's how to input invoices into QuickBooks and monitor their payments.

Inputting expenses and bills

Inputting Bills

Here's how to take note of a supplier bill you receive:

 ⊥ Introduce a new Bill.

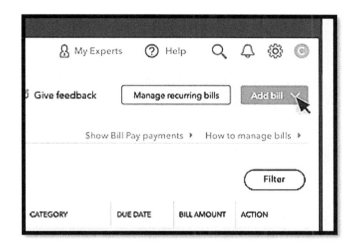

 ⊥ From the Supplier ▼menu, choose a supplier.
 ⊥ From the Terms ▼menu, choose the bill's terms. The provider expects payment at this point.
 ⊥ Enter the Bill No., Due Date, and Bill Date exactly as they appear on the bill.

 ⊥ Enter the bill information in the Category details box. From the Category menu, choose the spending account you use to record your transactions. Then provide a description.

- Include the amount and sales tax. The total amount shown depends on the selection made in the Amounts section.
- If you want to charge the customer for the expenditure, click the Billable option and enter their name in the Customer form.
- When you're done, choose Save and close.

Keep track of bill payments

There are two methods for recording bill payments. The following steps should be taken. If you paid the bill with cash or a credit card, use this method to keep track of both cash and credit card payments made toward a bill. You may either record each payment individually or all at once. Crucial: This is where you just record the accounting for your bill payments. Payments still need to be handled the way your provider has instructed:

Begin by opening Pay your bills

This shows all of the unpaid invoices you have entered into QuickBooks, along with their amounts and due dates. By default, it shows the last 365 days. To change the date range or look at a particular payee (supplier, for instance), click Filter.

To record payment on a bill:
- From the dropdown menu, choose the account you used to pay the bill. For instance, if you used your checking account to make the payment, choose chequing.
- **Suggestion:** Record payments for the same bill from several accounts (e.g., partly with a check and partially with a credit card) or make distinct entries on various days.
- If you choose a checking or savings account, you may enter the Beginning check number. This is something you can decide not to do.
- Enter the date of payment here.
- Check the boxes that match the invoices you have settled.
- Fill in the Payment box with the total amount you paid for each bill. Advice: In the Credit Applied column, you may enter any credit you may have with the provider.
- Select "Save" or "Save and close."

If you used a check to pay the bill, choose one of the following actions: Follow these procedures only if you paid with a check. This keeps QuickBooks accurate by documenting the payment in a certain manner:
- Launch a new check.
- From the Payee list, choose the provider you paid. This opens a window with all of their outstanding bills.

+ Click Add to attach an open bill with the cheque. Note: If you don't see this, click the little arrow next to the number. If you have credit with the provider, you may also add credit from the Credits section.
+ From the bank account drop-down option, choose the account you used to pay the check.
+ Enter the check's amount in the Amount area.
+ In the Outstanding Transactions column, choose the invoices to which the check payment was applied. Advice: If there are many expenses covered, check the boxes next to them. You may divide the payment and enter the amount for each bill in the Payment column.
+ Click Print Check or Print Expense Claim after selecting Print or Preview.
+ When you're done, choose Save and close or Save and new.

The expenses

QuickBooks Online makes it easy to keep track of company expenses in addition to tracking sales. Entering your income and costs gives you a more complete picture of your business's profits. If you have already paid for a business cost, enter it here. However, if you plan to pay for the spending later, include it as a bill. QuickBooks is instructed on how to record each transaction by these specific transaction types. **Here's how to record and monitor costs in QuickBooks.**

Document an expense

Use these procedures if you need to record a business cost in QuickBooks that you have previously paid for:
+ Select + New. Then choose Expense.
+ In the Payee column, click the supplier's name. Advice: Leave this box empty if the transaction covers more than one petty cash cost.
+ In the Payment Account section, choose the account you used to pay for the item.
+ In the Payment date field, enter the date of the cost.
+ Select the method of payment that you used to pay for it.
+ For more detailed tracking, provide a reference number. This is something you can decide not to do.
+ Type the cost data in the Category details field. From the Category menu, choose the spending account you use to record your transactions. Then provide a description. Advice: You may also enter specific products and services in the Item Details section to detail the cost.
+ Include the amount and sales tax.

- If you want to charge the client for the expenditure, choose the Billable checkbox and enter their name in the client or Customer/Project section.
- When you're done, choose Save and close.

Since you have already paid for the charges, you may alter them whenever you want in QuickBooks. **However, if you decide to charge your client for the expenditure, any modifications you make will have an impact on the invoice you give them later:**
- Select Expenses by navigating to it.
- Find the cost that needs revision. Select the View/Edit option in the Action column.
- Update the transaction as needed.
- Click Close after you've selected Save.

Follow the steps listed below to remove a cost that you have previously entered if you would want to erase it.
- Click on Expenses after navigating to it.
- Find the expenditure you want to eliminate. Select Delete from the View/Edit ▼ option in the Action column.
- Choose Delete to be sure you really want to delete the transaction.
- Erasing a cost keeps it visible in the audit record but removes it from reports.

The distinction between costs, checks, and bills

Learn how to pay bills that must be paid right now as well as those that must be paid later using bills, checks, or expenses. You may access them using the + New option in your QuickBooks Online account.

When should bills be entered?
- Enter supplier invoices to accurately reflect your accounts payable, especially if your reports are created on an accrual basis.
- If you are tracking supplier balances to find out how much you owe your suppliers, you will need to enter bills.
- Note a bill for any items or services you get and will pay for later, even if the provider does not provide an actual bill.
- For example, when you get your power bill, which is not due until the end of the month, use Bill to keep track of your bills. Next, generate the check and pay the bill using Pay Bills.

When to input bill payments:
- Choose Pay Bills to close a bill that you first placed into QuickBooks. To pay your bills, you may either print a check or use a credit card.
- A correct decrease in the Supplier balance is ensured when a bill is paid via Pay Bills.
- The bill may show up on your records as unpaid if you use expense or check.

- If you paid a bill electronically, please enter EFT in the box for the check number or initial check number.

When to record checks or expenditures:
- A transaction is simultaneously reported as a payment and an expense by the check and expense;
- While bills are for payables (received services or products to be paid later), checks and expenses are for services or items paid on the spot.
- Enter expenditure as a check instead of an expense if a check has to be produced.
- If you paid with a credit card, use Expense. If you paid by Electronic Fund Transfer (EFT), you should still use Cheque or Expense. You may put EFT in the "Check no." or "Ref no." fields.

For example, you should register the transaction using either Expense or Cheque if you bought items from Office Depot and paid for them immediately. Office Depot has no debt, thus you don't have to input or pay any invoices. Note: If the consumer selects "Print later" as their preferred delivery option, the cost will be recorded as a check. To confirm this, go through your customer's profile and choose Edit. Check the Payments section to make sure the preferred delivery method isn't set to print later.

Process for Accounts Payable

There are several facets of accounting to keep an eye on beyond budgeting and figure calculation. The accounts payable process is one of the most important ones. "Accounts payable" is the phrase used to describe the various amounts that your business owes to external suppliers for goods and services that you haven't yet paid for, including credit card transactions, production costs, inventory, and repair services. Accounts payable, or AP, is the total amount of money you owe other businesses for products or services they billed you for. One could think, where can I find accounts payable? The obligations related to your company's accounts payable are included in the current liabilities section of your balance sheet. These amounts are classified as short-term loans rather than long-term debt, such as a company loan. Accounts payable only applies to businesses that use the accrual method of accounting, not cash-based accounting. The accrual system of accounting records revenue and expenses as soon as they are billed and paid, which explains why this is the case. Accrual accounting employs invoice processing to buy and provide services on a credit or debit basis, instead than demanding payment right away. Payment for the commodity or service must normally be made within 30 days of the supplier's invoice date. Let's look at an example of how the accounts payable process works. In this case, imagine that you are the proprietor of the restaurant and that you would want to purchase fresh tomatoes from a local food supplier.

- Your restaurant places an order for 100 pounds of tomatoes, which comes to a total of $100.
- The food supplier sends you an invoice for $100, complete with conditions and a payment deadline.
- You add the whole $100 amount outstanding to your accounts payable.
- After your restaurant pays the supplier, the amount is deducted from your accounts payable and $100 is taken out of your cash flow.

Why is the account payable procedure so crucial?

In a number of ways, the accounts payable process is essential to your business's accounting processes.

- **Cash flow:** A list of all your debts and the individuals you owe them to will help you better manage your company's finances. 56% of firms have trouble estimating their cash flow because of AP issues. Gaining more knowledge can make it easier for you to pay off your debts, organize your spending and money, and prevent blunders.
- **Handling debt:** Paying your bills is essential, regardless of whether they are personal or business-related. Monitoring and paying suppliers on time is another way to cultivate positive supplier relationships. After all, no one likes a long-standing IOU.
- **Savings:** Some vendors provide early payment incentives for on-time payments, while others impose late penalties for payments received after the deadline. In any event, keeping track of your due amounts may help you save money and save headache.
- **Historical documents:** Using AP to store invoice data not only gives organizational piece of mind, but it also helps provide a precise picture of the transaction history. It may be simpler for you to identify and deal with spending issues if you maintain a thorough record of your outgoing payments. A thorough audit trail may also significantly increase the effectiveness of audits conducted by tax agencies, external parties, and internal parties.

Easy methods for efficiently handling accounts payable

So, how is the procedure of accounts payable implemented? These are the five fundamental phases that make up the accounts payable workflow:

- **Provide supplier information:** This step may help you better organize your orders, payment deadlines, and contact information. The due dates for supplier payments may be indicated by codes like net 10, 30, and 60. Payment must be made within 10 days after the purchase date, 30 days after the purchase date, and so on.

- **Approval of the invoice:** Before beginning the payment process, confirm that the goods or service you requested has been delivered and verify the correctness of your invoice.
- **Handle the payment of unpaid invoices:** After you've verified that your invoices are correct, you may begin paying the appropriate suppliers. Depending on your payment method and the supplier's preferences, you may need to notify them that money is on its way.
- **Record and play again:** It's time to add the most current data to your books after finishing steps 1-4. The process of reconciliation may be automated using accounting software. After a supplier payment has been received, you may remove it from your list of accounts payable. Repeat the process once per week.

Utilize QuickBooks to automate the accounts payable procedure

The success of your small company largely depends on a number of aspects, such as generating leads, identifying talent, and achieving creative objectives. The accounts payable method must be included for effective company accounting, but it might be challenging to complete since there are only 24 hours in a day. With QuickBooks, you can automate expenditure control and go back to your favorite parts of managing your business. Whether you're working hard on a construction site or impressing customers and landing contracts, having more time provides you more influence over your course.

With QuickBooks, you can securely arrange and handle your invoices online:
- You always pay your bills on time since they are all in one place.
- QuickBooks automatically tracks and records bills paid by check or direct deposit, which reduces errors.
- Pay your bills using the method that works best for you and your suppliers: debit cards or free bank transfers are good choices, but your supplier may also accept payments by direct deposit or paper check.
- When using a credit card, you may decide to postpone invoices or make partial bill payments to prolong your cash flow.
- Scalable, automated processes put you in a successful position and save you time. Online process automation reduces the need for paperless invoicing.
- Gaining more insight into your company's expenditures increases its efficiency.

Keeping tabs on supplier transactions and handling payables

Transactions with vendors

Learn how to review and edit vendor transactions using QuickBooks Online. To see the transactions of suppliers, do the activities listed below:

- Select Expenses and then Navigate to Vendors.
- Find and choose your preferred seller.
- Every transaction for this vendor should be visible to you under the Transaction List.

Take the actions listed below to handle the data about your vendors: Once you've selected a vendor, you may manage and change their profile and transactions.

- Click Edit to modify the vendor's profile.
- Choose New Transaction to create a new vendor credit, bill, expenditure, check, or purchase order for that vendor.
- To see just certain types of transactions, use the Filter ▼ option.
- Click the Printer button to print the vendor transactions.
- **After selecting the specific transactions, utilize the Batch operations ▼ menu to:**
  - Pay the specified bills online
  - Sort the chosen transactions into categories.
  - Transactions that are null and void
  - Print the transactions.
- To export the vendor transactions to an Excel spreadsheet, use the Export icon. **You also decide to use the procedures below to verify the vendor's money bar;** The vibrant bar in the vendor's window is the money bar. With it, you can get a visual overview of every contact you have with your vendor. It shows the following items' amounts and sums:
- You have open purchase orders with suppliers.
- The quantity of past-due invoices and vendor bills
- Invoices that is due within the previous 30 days

Handling Payables

When an invoice is sent to you over the QuickBooks Business Network, QuickBooks may recognize the vendor information and notify you of it on the Bills page. You may then promptly review and approve the charge to have it immediately recorded in your records. Accounts payable (AP) automation reduces the possibility of mistakes resulting from manual input and saves you time when creating and paying your invoices. Note:

Although it may not be accessible in all accounts at this time, this functionality will be available to QuickBooks Simple Start, QuickBooks Online Essentials, QuickBooks Online Plus, and QuickBooks Online Advanced accounts. When you get an invoice from another QuickBooks user, review the contents and make arrangements for payment, or submit the bill to QuickBooks for payment at a later time.

- Access your QuickBooks Online account by logging in.
- Go to Bills after Expenses.
- Select the option that says "For review."
- From the list of pending legislation, choose the Review bill.
- The bill on the new screen shows data extracted from the invoice.
- Select Account or Category.
- Verify the data and make any required corrections.
- Next, choose Save and schedule payment or Save and close. If you would rather not have this bill included, choose Delete this bill.

You may browse, manage, and, if you haven't already, record payments for the bill after it have been protected. The invoice comes with a PDF version in case you wish to review it at a later time. AP Automation collects data from bills as you submit them and creates the transaction automatically to add to QuickBooks.

To upload invoices,

- Log in to your QuickBooks Online account.
- After expenses, go to bills. From the Add Bill ▼dropdown menu, choose Upload from the computer.
- You may drag and drop files into the Upload box or click the Upload button to choose files from your computer. Note: QuickBooks supports the following image formats: PDF, JPEG, JPG, GIF, and PNG.
- You may now examine the bill's information, schedule a payment time, or pay later on the "For review" page.

Comprehending Financial Reporting

Financial reporting is the process of documenting and disseminating financial performance and activity across certain time periods, often quarterly or yearly. Businesses use financial reports to organize accounting data and provide a summary of their current financial status. The public may examine a large number of financial reports, which are essential for forecasting future development, profitability, and industry position. A few key statements should be used when reporting financial data. Many significant financial reporting objectives are satisfied by the information you provide in these documents.

- Monitoring the flow of funds
- Assessing the value of assets and liabilities

- Examining the stock held by shareholders
- Assessing financial success

Financial reporting is crucial because it facilitates the following goals:

Keeping an eye on earnings and spending

The task of monitoring revenue and spending is also greatly aided by financial reporting. Monitoring financial records helps you identify key areas of spending and is necessary for effective debt management and planning. Organizations must regularly track their revenue and spending in order to preserve transparency in fiercely competitive markets. You can thus monitor current assets and liabilities via paperwork thanks to financial reporting. Accurate financial documentation is also necessary to measure critical performance metrics, such debt-to-asset ratios, which investors use to evaluate how successfully companies generate revenue and settle debt.

Aids in guaranteeing adherence

Financial reporting is one of the procedures that companies must follow in order to comply with accounting requirements. Every document you use to evaluate financial operations is examined by a number of financial regulatory bodies. Therefore, accurate documentation is necessary to guarantee that all financial reports adhere to tax regulations and financial reporting requirements. Accurate financial records also expedite tax, appraisal, and audit processes, reducing the time needed to meet critical financial obligations and improving the guarantee of financial compliance.

Conveys crucial information

To plan budgets, assess performance, and make decisions, professionals, executives, investors, and important shareholders all depend on current financial data. Transparency and open communication are essential for financial assessments, investment possibilities, and funding. Many creditors and investors use the information that companies publish in their financial statements to assess profitability, risk, and future returns.

Provide assistance with financial analysis and judgment

Accounting data is necessary for analysis to support business decisions. Financial statements improve accountability and make it easier to examine significant financial data. Documents like the income statement and balance sheet provide you access to real-time data that you can use to track historical performance, identify key spending areas, and enhance forecasts. Reporting helps businesses evaluate their current operations and make choices about future development in two ways: via improved data models and comprehensive financial analysis.

The many forms of financial reporting are listed below:

- **Balance sheet:** This document shows your current total assets, liabilities, and equity. By examining the balance sheet, you may rapidly ascertain the total assets, minus the equity and liabilities. Companies often keep a quarterly eye on their balance sheets, and they may use the data to produce yearly reports. Balance sheets may also be used to evaluate your current asset liquidity and debt coverage in real time.

- **Income statement:** While the balance sheet assesses current activities, the income sheet records these operations over a longer time frame. Some businesses maintain quarterly income statement records, which they use to monitor their financial operations throughout the year. The income statement shows revenue, net income, expenses, and profits per capital share, if a business decides to list its shares on the stock market. Businesses utilize the income statement, also referred to as the profit-and-loss statement or P&L statement, to report their profits and losses.

- A key instrument for evaluating how successfully companies generate cash flow to pay down debt is the cash flow statement. The amount that businesses fund their operations and investments is also included in the documentation of cash flow, which shows the ongoing activities that generate revenue to pay expenses. Accurate cash flow data is necessary to comprehend the efficacy of current practices, expenditure trends, and revenue generation.

- The cash flow statement also gives investors a lot of information about how risky an investment a firm is. The cash flow statement typically consists of three primary **parts, as opposed to the income statement and balance sheet, which additionally need computations to record financial values:**

  - ➤ The main investment operations include extending loans or credit, selling assets, producing and using investment profits, and paying out from mergers or acquisitions. The operational chores include cash receipts, wages, income tax, inventory, and accounts receivable and payments.

  - ➤ Activities pertaining to secondary investments, such purchasing fixed assets for offices, real estate, or equipment

  - ➤ Financing activities, including cash payments to investors, cash payments to shareholders, debt repayment and issuance, stock buybacks, and dividends that are due

Financial reporting is an essential process in almost every sector. Businesses and enterprises depend on the review and analysis of financial information to make decisions and get finance. Financial firms also utilize financial paperwork to monitor compliance, provide loans, and assess profitability and performance. **Take a look at the following organizations and occupations that use financial reports:**

+ **Investors, owners, and creditors:** Investors and shareholders own firm stock and look at financial statements to assess how lucrative operations are. Creditors also use information from financial reports to determine how well-run companies are at paying back debt and extending loans to support growth.

+ **Executive supervisors:** Using financial reporting tools, teams and executive directors evaluate performance and update relevant paperwork. Financial reporting also supports executive decision-making, which companies use to establish departmental goals and objectives.

+ **Organizations that oversee regulations:** These firms also gather and analyze company data from financial reports. Two government agencies that monitor financial reporting procedures pertaining to tax and revenue documentation are the Securities Exchange Commission (SEC) and the Internal Revenue Service (IRS).

+ **Customers in the sector:** In order to promote market openness and educate consumers about how businesses operate, financial reporting is essential. By educating consumers, open disclosure of profits, investment activities, and philanthropic contributions may boost sales.

Producing and personalizing financial statements

QuickBooks Desktop offers a variety of integrated financial reports that allow you to see different aspects of your business's performance. These reports may also be customized to meet the unique needs of the business.

Details of the balance sheet and profit & loss reports

To help you rapidly evaluate the status of your business, a number of pre-custom reports are available. Some of the more popular ones are as follows: Unlike the P&L summary report, which just shows totals, this report shows year-to-date (YTD) transactions for each income and expenditure account.

By default,

+ QuickBooks compresses the amounts for each item with multiple amounts into a single number and displays the modifications column, which indicates whether any human adjustments have been made to an account. The report is simpler to publish when it is condensed in this way.

Take note: The default date range is current fiscal year up to this point. You may show the profit and loss for a different set of dates if you choose one from the Dates menu.

- To start the report, choose Company & Financial > Profit & Loss Detail from the Reports menu.

Detail Report on the Balance Sheet

This report is an enlarged version of the Balance Sheet Standard report. The beginning balance from the previous month, the transactions done in the account so far this month, and the ending balance as of today are all shown in the report for each account. As with earlier Balance Sheet reports, this one calculates your company's worth by subtracting all of its obligations from all of its assets. The result is the equity of your firm, or the value of your company.

By default:

- It displays the adjustments column, which indicates whether an account has undergone any human modifications.
- It is compressed, which means that QuickBooks reduces each item's many quantities to a single value. The report is simpler to publish when it is condensed in this way.
- To begin this report, choose Company & Financial > Balance Sheet Detail from the Reports menu.

Foreign currency in the balance sheet or profit and loss report

It should be mentioned that QuickBooks can currently only produce a balance sheet and profit and loss report in the user's native currency. These reports translate foreign currency transactions into their comparable amounts in US dollars. **For the following summary reports, however, you may choose to show values in either your local currency (which is the default) or international amounts:**

- A/R Aging
- A/P Aging
- Customer Balance Summary
- Vendor Balance Summary
- Sales by Customer Summary
- Purchases by Vendor Summary (if purchase orders are turned on)

To change the default currency of one of these summary reports:

- Select "Customize Report."
- After choosing the Display tab, click the "Display amounts in" box.

88

- ➢ You have the option to see the amount in the foreign transaction currency or only in your native currency.
- ➢ Click "OK."
- ✦ To save the report, choose Memorize.

Profit and Loss Comparison Report for Several Years

Follow the steps below to get a profit and loss report that displays yearly data separated into columns for easy comparison.

- ✦ From the Reports menu, choose Company & Financial > Profit & Loss Standard.
- ✦ Select "Customize Report."
- ✦ **Choose the tab for Display.**
    - ➢ In the form and to date fields, enter the years you would want to see on the report.
    - ➢ Using the dropdown menu, choose the year from the Display columns.
- ✦ Select OK.

Making use of dashboards to get insights in real time

At its core, QuickBooks' dashboard feature acts as a single spot for all financial activities and the required management tools. When you enter into QuickBooks, the dashboard is the first screen you see and provides crucial glimpses into your company's financial situation. With a variety of widgets and modules available, it's a personalized canvas for the well-being of your company. Important financial questions like "Is my business profitable?" and "How am I doing compared to last year?" are meant to be quickly answered via dashboards. QuickBooks dashboard transparency extends beyond straightforward expense and revenue monitoring to provide insights that facilitate informed decision-making.

Important Aspects and Perspectives

QuickBooks dashboards provide a feature set that extends well beyond basic accounting. **QuickBooks dashboards may help you keep an eye on your company's financial health in the following ways:**

- ✦ **Financial Data Visualizations:** Graphs, charts, and other visual representations of your financial data are more than just eye candy; they speed up your comprehension of the information and decision-making. All of these visualizations, which include income comparisons and balance sheets, are easily accessible from your dashboard.

- **Customization Options:** QuickBooks understands the need of tailored insights since every business is unique. Widgets on customized dashboards may be resized and rearranged to create a layout that meets your company's specific financial needs.

Advantages for Entrepreneurs

The company's core is its financial health, and QuickBooks dashboards provide crucial tools to support it. These consist of:

- **Real-Time Monitoring:** One of the fundamental principles of business is the prompt resolution of pressing issues. With QuickBooks' real-time updating, you'll never miss any big financial changes—whether it's an unexpected spending or a surge in sales.
- **Making Informed Decisions:** QuickBooks dashboards are a useful tool for making data-driven decisions. If you have access to real-time data, historical patterns, and forecasting tools, you can make well-informed choices that support your company's strategic goals.
- **Better financial management:** The insights and data accuracy of QuickBooks dashboards improve financing management. QuickBooks gives you the resources you need to optimize your business's financial operations, whether that means detecting and fixing inefficiencies or improving cash flow management.

Advice for Using the Dashboard Effectively

Simply having access to QuickBooks dashboards is insufficient; what really makes them helpful is how thoughtfully and effectively they can be used:

- **Establishing Goals and KPIs:** Dashboards are most effective when they align with your organization's goals. In QuickBooks, setting Key Performance Indicators (KPIs) helps you ensure that the dashboard achieves your objectives.
- **Consistency is crucial in regular monitoring and analysis.** Regularly monitoring your QuickBooks dashboard helps you stay informed and adaptable. Additionally, possibilities, trends, and blind spots may be revealed by routine data analysis.

The decisions you make with your dashboard will determine how helpful it is. Utilize the data on your QuickBooks dashboard to plan, strategize, and anticipate the future. Act proactively rather than reactively, and your business will thank you for it. QuickBooks dashboards are business companions who assist you in managing the financial tides of your organization. They are not just financial instruments. You can remain ahead of the curve and have the insight and foresight required guiding your business toward success by depending on QuickBooks. Your quiet but immensely helpful partners in a fast-paced sector where adaptability and judgment are essential are QuickBooks dashboards. They are more than simply a software feature; they are a commitment to your business's financial health, a handshake with data-driven leadership, and a contract with advancement. Improve company management by using QuickBooks dashboards to uncover the potential buried in your data.

Reports are shared and exported for stakeholders

Quality reporting should be a required part of any board development strategy. Stakeholder reports facilitate stakeholder participation and effective board governance. By creating reports for stakeholders, a board may maintain good ties with them and inform them of the company's performance and success metrics. Additionally, reporting after a consultation lets stakeholders know what the board has done to address the concerns brought up. The stakeholder reporting process has three primary objectives: trust, accountability, and openness. **Some common benefits of reporting to a stakeholder include the following:**

- Through transparency, it enables better stakeholder/board relations.
- It provides accountability, which helps to keep the data, measurements, and plan all on track.
- It makes it easier for stakeholders and the board to build trust, which is a prerequisite for fruitful collaboration and organizational growth.

The opportunity to clearly outline the company's present performance and the steps that must be taken to complete the required tasks is one of the less obvious advantages of reporting to stakeholders. As such, it encourages commitment and makes it easier for the board and stakeholders to form fruitful collaborations. **Regular reporting to stakeholders also has the following benefits:**

- Increasing the ties between the stakeholders and the board
- Creating a collaborative atmosphere founded on openness, responsibility, and confidence
- Including employees and other internal stakeholders
- Support from stakeholders for the company's growth and development
- Encouraging environmentally and socially responsible behavior (which might attract investors)
- Promoting more involvement from interested parties
- Maintaining a brand's reputation
- Improving the governance of corporations

Other accountants on your team may access and share the personalized reports you create. At the moment, custom reports may only be kept private for the creator or sent to the whole accounting team.

How to provide your employees with corporate reports

Seeing and controlling personalized reports

- Go to the Custom Reports tab after selecting the Reports option in QuickBooks Online Accountant.
- Choose a custom report to see.

To export a customized report to Excel or a PDF:

- Find the customized report.
- Select the dropdown ▼ option in the Action column.
- Select Export as PDF or Export as Excel.

Distribute personalized reports

Once a report is completely personalized, you decide who should see it. To share your firm's report, do the actions listed below:

- Navigate to QuickBooks Online Accountant's Reports menu.
- Use these procedures to customize a report.
- Make the decision to preserve the personalization.
- To share it with everyone at your firm, choose All from the Share with option. If you would rather to keep it private, select None. Important: You cannot change your mind after you choose All.
- Click "Save."

Practice Exercises

- Keep track of your earnings.
- Produce sales receipts and invoices.
- Oversee client transactions and monitor payments.
- Add costs and bills.
- Manage payables and keep tabs on vendor transactions.
- Create and modify financial summaries.
- Use dashboards to get information in real time.

CHAPTER FOUR
ADVANCED TOOLS AND FEATURES
Business Process Automation

By 2025, 80 percent of companies will use intelligent automation. Therefore, automating processes is now a critical step for CIOs to fully embrace digital transformation and future-proof their enterprises. Businesses may improve efficiency, simplify processes, and develop new business models with the aid of business process automation. Unfortunately, for a number of reasons, including inadequate planning, reluctance to change, high implementation costs, and technological challenges, over 90% of automation attempts fail. Business automation, also known as business process automation, uses technology to automate internal organizational operations and procedures. It may assist a company in converting its manual procedures into universally adopted automated ones, which can lead to significant increases in production. The main objectives of BPA are to improve operational efficiency, reduce mistakes, standardize processes, and free up employees to concentrate on more strategically significant work. By automating these repetitive tasks, businesses may significantly reduce costs and increase efficiency, improving overall performance. You will discover many methods for efficiently automating business procedures in QuickBooks in the sections that follow.

Configuring reminders and recurring transactions

With QuickBooks Online, you may create templates for regular transactions, such reoccurring spending. You may do this for any transaction, with the exception of time-related tasks and bill payments. Configuring and optimizing recurring templates will be covered.

Establish a fresh recurring template

+ Go to the Settings ⚙.
+ Under Lists, choose Recurring Transactions.

↓ Select New.

↓ Click OK after selecting the preferred transaction type.

↓ Enter the template's name here.
↓ Select a type: Reminder, Scheduled, or Unscheduled.
↓ After filling up the boxes, choose "Save template."

Use the steps listed below to make an existing transaction recurring in the new experience:

↓ Access an already open transaction.
↓ Choose Make Recurring (or Enable Recurring Payments) from the form's footer to build a template. If you opened an invoice, choose Automation and then Recurring invoice.

Recurring estimates are not possible with the new estimate and invoicing experience. Go back to the earlier case to estimate a recurrent transaction. **To make an existing transaction recurring in the previous experience, follow these steps:**

- Access an already open transaction.
- Choose Make Recurring (or Enable Recurring Payments) from the form's footer to build a template.

By accessing pre-existing duplicate templates, you may also decide to create templates more quickly.

- Go to the Settings ⬚ .
- Select Recurring Transactions.
- In the Action column, choose Duplicate from the Edit▼ dropdown box. All parameters will be present in the duplicate copy, with the exception of the title.

Making use of automated processes to increase productivity

The way businesses manage their financial operations is being revolutionized by QuickBooks Workflow Automation. Automating repetitive activities may help businesses save time, reduce mistakes, and increase overall efficiency. Businesses may streamline their operations and focus on client satisfaction and expansion instead of tedious accounting tasks with the aid of this powerful technology.

- Automate invoice and payment reminders.
- Make monitoring and reporting of spending easier.
- Simple integration with other business tools
- Enhance the data's correctness and consistency.

One of its most noteworthy features is the ability to integrate QuickBooks Workflow Automation with a number of services, including ApiX-Drive. This connection platform makes it simple for businesses to integrate QuickBooks with other applications, ensuring a smooth data movement across systems. By using these connectors, businesses may further enhance process automation, thus solidifying QuickBooks' position as an essential tool for modern corporate operations.

Finding and optimizing processes

Procedures in QuickBooks need to be defined and refined in order to boost productivity and reduce human error rates. Create a map of every procedure that is presently in use, such as billing and payroll processing. Identify the repetitive tasks that use the most time and resources. After these processes are well documented, rank them in order of impact on company operations. This ensures a smoother transition and faster results by allowing you to focus on automating the most crucial processes first. To maximize these processes, consider integrating QuickBooks with other business technology using platforms such as ApiX-Drive. ApiX-Drive makes it easier and requires less technical expertise to connect QuickBooks with email marketing providers, CRM programs, and other essential tools. By automating data transfer and synchronization across several platforms, you may reduce mistakes, eliminate unnecessary data input, and free up valuable time for more essential tasks. This comprehensive approach increases productivity and ensures that your financial data is up-to-date and correct.

Making Use of QuickBooks Automation Tools

QuickBooks offers a wide range of automation tools to help you streamline your accounting processes and save time. By using this technology, businesses may enhance efficiency and reduce the likelihood of human error.

- **Automated Invoicing:** To ensure correct billing and consistent cash flow, you may set up recurring invoices in QuickBooks.
- By linking your credit cards and bank accounts, expense monitoring automatically imports and categorizes your transactions, making expenditure management simpler.
- **Payroll Automation:** Automate payroll calculations, tax filings, and direct payments to ensure accuracy and compliance.

By adopting QuickBooks automation solutions to handle repetitive tasks, businesses can focus more on strategic operations. Tools like ApiX-Drive, which provide smooth software interaction, provide an efficient and user-friendly workflow, hence enhancing QuickBooks' performance. To expedite your accounting processes and promote business growth, embrace these automation alternatives.

Automating routine accounting duties

Automating repetitive accounting tasks using QuickBooks may significantly improve productivity and accuracy. By using process automation, businesses may reduce mistakes, ensure timely financial reporting, and restrict human data input. Accountants may now focus on more strategic projects because of the time savings. One of the key benefits of automation is its seamless connection with a variety of financial tools and services. For instance, utilizing platforms like ApiX-Drive, businesses can easily integrate QuickBooks with other applications, ensuring smooth data flow and synchronization. This eliminates the need for time-consuming manual procedures and provides real-time updates across several platforms. By automating certain standard accounting procedures, businesses can maintain accurate financial records and boost overall efficiency. Additionally, the integration capabilities of some systems ensure that data is consistently up-to-date, providing a reliable foundation for financial decision-making.

Advantages and Difficulties of Automating QuickBooks Workflow

Enhanced accuracy and efficiency in financial operations are just two of the numerous benefits of using QuickBooks Workflow Automation. By automating repetitive tasks, businesses may reduce human error and save time. As a consequence, financial reporting will be more precise and employees may now focus on higher-value tasks. Additionally, connecting QuickBooks with other tools via specific services may further optimize procedures by ensuring seamless data transfer and synchronization across several platforms. However, there are challenges to consider when putting QuickBooks Workflow Automation into practice. One of the biggest obstacles is the initial setup and customization, which may be time-consuming and need technical expertise. Employers must also ensure that staff members are adequately educated to use the new automated technology. Finally, processes need to be regularly reviewed and adjusted to reflect changes in business practices or regulatory requirements, even though automation may significantly reduce mistakes.

Using QuickBooks Online for Payroll Management

Payroll administration includes calculating employee hours, paying employees, deducting taxes, and monitoring your business's financial records. Payroll administration, which includes processing sensitive employee data, calculating taxes, and paying workers' bank accounts, may be challenging and dangerous. Understanding the right payroll administration strategies is essential to preserving legal compliance. If payroll cannot be handled, you are unable to pay workers. Without employees, your business cannot function. Employees want to get paid on time, and if you can't manage payroll efficiently, you might lose important team members and perhaps break the law.

The primary arguments for why your business must properly manage payroll are as follows:

- **Legal requirements:** Both federal and state governments have rules and regulations pertaining to payroll tax filing. If you don't file on time, you might be subject to harsh fines or penalties. Once again, if you make a mistake about an employee's pay and don't fix it, you are responsible. It is important to maintain as much conformity as possible.
- **Employee loyalty:** If you are unable to pay your superstar team members on time or appropriately, they are unlikely to remain on your team. Strong employees

could look for other job, so it's important to retain them and make sure their pay is consistently made on time and precisely.

- ᛒ **Employee efficiency:** It's not just about keeping your employees on board; you want them to thrive and perform well. If you can retain them, which is doubtful, underpaying them may cause them to become disengaged or look for other work, which would reduce production.
- ᛒ **Finance for businesses:** Your budget may suffer as a result of poor payroll administration. You could think you have more money in your bank account than you really have which might lead to missed checks or bank fees in addition to paying a fine.

Payroll administration is one of the most important administrative duties for the whole business. If done correctly, it will mostly go undetected; yet, if done incorrectly, it might stop the firm from operating.

Setting up compliance parameters and payroll features

Does your printer need to be oriented in order to print pay stubs or your chart of accounts? **You may modify these and other parameters using payroll options:**

- ᛒ Go to the Settings ⬚.
- ᛒ Press the Payroll Settings button.
- ᛒ **From the Setup Overview page, you may visit many windows to customize the following information:**
  - ➢ Pay rules (such vacation and salary schedules)
  - ➢ Tax Setup (information required to ensure that taxes are appropriately gathered and processed)
  - ➢ Deductions (common information for all workers, such as health insurance and retirement schemes)
  - ➢ Preferences (for choosing accounting and check printing choices)

Reminder: Items that you define here, such pay policies and deductions, will be accessible as default options when you set up your workers. When you add employees, they may also be configured. You will be asked a number of questions to help you along the way, but in the end, the choice is yours. If you want to set those steps up when you add the employee, you may skip them in this instruction.

- ᛒ In the Setup Overview screen's Company and Account section, choose Accounting.
- ᛒ In the Accounting Preferences tab, create new accounts to track payroll expenses. If the account you want to use is not in the drop-down list, you will have to add it to the Chart of Accounts.
- ᛒ Click "OK."

Managing employee benefits and processing paychecks

Payroll may save you time if you include employee benefits. Payroll perks in Advanced Payroll provide advantages such as dispersing the benefit's cash value evenly across the tax year. This amount is added to the employee's taxable salary for each period, as seen on their paystubs.

Activate the payrolling features

‡ Go to Payroll and then Payroll Settings.

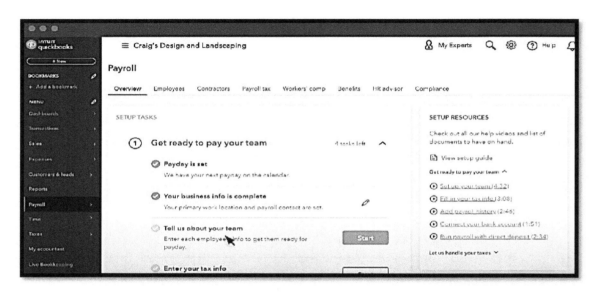

‡ From the Pay Run Settings menu, choose the Benefit Categories

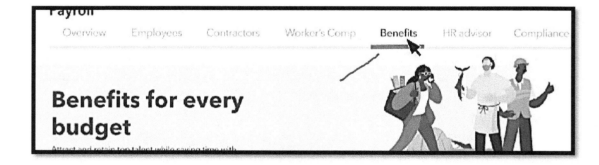

‡ Click the arrow next to processing options to see more information.
‡ Navigate to Payrolling.

- Select the tax year that your business was set up.
- Select "Save."

Include a benefit category

- Press Add.
- The advantage will start when you choose the year.
- If you want to roll over the benefit into the next tax year, check this option.
- Once the benefit type has been selected, fill out the appropriate forms.
- Click "Save."
- To modify the benefit category, click the pencil symbol. To make sure it's gone, click the trash can icon and choose Delete.

Connect the benefit category to the workers

- Proceed to Payroll and choose the Employees area.

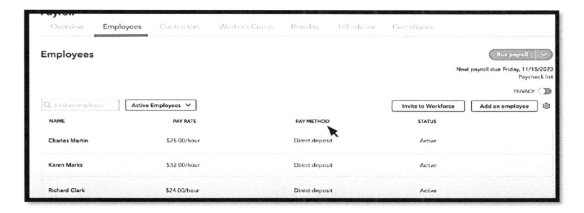

- Selecting the employee's name will allow you to access their profile.
- Select the Benefits.
- Press Add.
- Choose the benefit category.
- Provide the pertinent information in the benefit type areas.
- Click "Save."

Provide an advantage to diverse staff

You may save time and make sure that everyone gets their benefits by linking benefits to many workers.

Note: To add automobile benefits, only the employee record should be utilized.
- After choosing Payroll, choose Payroll Settings.
- It is necessary to choose Benefit Categories in Pay Run Settings.
- In the Benefits section, choose the link that says "No linked employees" next to the perk.
- Find the employees you want to link to the benefit.
- Press Add.
- Click "Save."

Set up the pro-rata computation

The pro-rata calculation method, which considers an employee's start and finish dates, may be used to calculate their appropriate share of benefits. It helps ensure that employees may only get benefits while they are employed.
- Locate and click on Pro-rata.
- Please specify the start and end dates for the employee.
- The calculator will show you the revised pro-rata yearly cost based on the dates you entered.
- If the sum is acceptable to you, choose Use new pro-rata. This will automatically update when you save.
- Uncheck the box and enter the desired amount if you would want to provide your value.
- You may automate the required calculations when payroll is conducted by setting the pro-rata on the first pay run.
- The calculation is performed by dividing the total number of pay periods remaining by the remaining cash equivalent, minus the amount that has already been paid, for pay runs that follow the first.
- If you provide an end date, the calculation will account for the benefit's length and stop doing so when the designated date has passed.

Making the move to Advanced Payroll

If, in the midst of the tax year, you switched to QuickBooks Online Advanced Payroll and now need to add benefits that were previously managed by another payroll system, don't freak out. It's still okay to incorporate them. **The following procedures may be used to add year-to-date earnings amounts; transfer over current leave balances, and input opening balances when switching payroll systems:**
- After selecting Payroll, you should pick Payroll Settings.
- From the Business Settings menu, choose Opening Balances.
- Select the current fiscal year.

+ Click "Save."

It is therefore necessary to add the total amount that has already been paid to workers for these perks. **Here's how to accomplish that:**
+ Go to the employee's page.
+ Select the Opening Balances tab.
+ Select the choice for profits.
+ Enter the amounts.
+ Click "Save."

Once payroll processing is finished, the benefits will appear on the employee's payslip and be included in their taxable pay.

Terminate a worker who receives payroll benefits

Care must be taken when firing a worker who gets paid time off. You should be aware of the following:
+ **Date of termination:** Ensure that an employee is let go within their most recent pay period. This will ensure that any outstanding balances for tax-exempt benefits are reflected. Since most benefits are provided for a full year, the leftover funds will be added to the final pay and used to calculate taxes. A report on these values will be sent to HMRC.
+ **Taxable pay:** If the whole amount cannot be taxed in the last pay period, HMRC will be notified of the taxable pay received and will handle any tax owed directly with the employee.
+ **Termination of benefits:** If an employee's benefits expire at the same time as their leave of absence, you must terminate them. Change the pro-rata dates, benefit date available, or cost from the employee's profile to compute the amount owed. The update will be shown in the pay run. Remember that if an employee has payrolled benefits, you cannot postpone their termination date beyond the end of the current pay month.
+ **Payrolled benefits and termination:** An employee's payrolled benefits will not be impacted if they are fired using the Terminate option on their employee profile. Any outstanding amounts for these benefits must be submitted to HMRC separately, outside of QuickBooks.

Inventory Control and Monitoring

Inventory management is essential for every business that deals with physical goods. From the time of receipt until the point of sale, it outlines the process for monitoring and managing stock levels. Here, we'll look at the importance of inventory monitoring along with some of its benefits and drawbacks. One of the biggest benefits of inventory management for your company is the ability to prevent stockouts. This irritates customers, and if they go elsewhere for what they need, it can lose them business. By keeping an eye on inventory levels and demand, you can ensure that they have adequate merchandise on hand without accumulating surplus inventory that might tie up finances and take up valuable space. Monitoring your inventory can help you better manage your cash flow. By keeping accurate records of inventory prices and levels, you may make well-informed decisions about when and how much new inventory to purchase. In addition to helping businesses avoid tying up too much cash in inventory, this may guarantee that they have enough items on hand to satisfy customer demand. By keeping an eye on demand and inventory levels, businesses may see trends and patterns in customer behavior. Pricing, promotions, and ordering choices may all be influenced by this data. Businesses may also use this to streamline their inventory management processes and boost overall efficiency. In order for businesses to comply with legal and regulatory obligations, inventory monitoring is also crucial. For instance, businesses that deal with perishable commodities could be obliged to maintain detailed records of their inventory levels and expiry dates to ensure they are not selling customers outdated goods. By using inventory monitoring software or systems, you may ensure that you are following industry standards and avoiding legal issues.

Controlling product listings and inventory levels

QuickBooks Online has everything you need to manage your inventory. Get information about what you sell and purchase, monitor your inventory, and get notifications when it's time to restock. You may also put non-inventory products and services here to quickly add them to your sales forms. Inventory capabilities are available in more advanced versions of QuickBooks Online. If you haven't already, upgrade to QuickBooks Plus or Advanced to start monitoring your inventory.

Turn on inventory tracking

If you haven't previously, turn these settings on so you can add your inventory.
- Click the Settings gear icon to choose Account and Settings.
- Select the tab for sales.

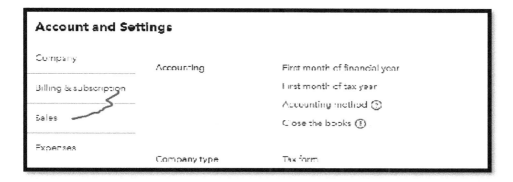

- Choose Edit under Products and Services.
- Turn on the Show Product/Service column on the sales form.
- You may also activate price rules if you decide to use variable pricing for your products.
- Turn on the tools that monitor available inventory levels, price/rate, and quantity.
- Click Done after selecting Save.

Add goods from the inventory

In addition to your inventory items, you may also add additional products and services you offer into QuickBooks. This allows you to quickly add them as line items to your sales forms. The steps for adding inventory, non-inventory, and service goods differ slightly: To add inventory items, follow these steps. You are able to regulate and keep an eye on product quantities since you sell these things.

- After selecting Settings, choose Products & Services.
- Once you've selected New, choose Inventory.

- Enter the required data, including the SKU and name.

After completing the aforementioned settings, you may proceed to the following actions:
- Stock the starting amount of your merchandise. Next, enter the date you started recording that number in the As of date field.
- Add a reorder point so that you may be notified when it's time to make another purchase.
- After choosing the Inventory Asset account, pick Inventory Asset from the dropdown menu. QuickBooks uses this account to keep track of the cost or inventory value of every item you own.

Footnote: Depending on when you wish to start monitoring your company, you may have different amounts on hand at first. For example, if you wish to start monitoring at the beginning of your fiscal year, enter the quantities of your items at that time.

However, if you add a new product from a seller, put "0" for the product's initial quantity. Note how much of this product the merchants send you after saving. This ensures that the initial sum won't be doubled. Additionally, make sure that you include goods and services that you sell or purchase but do not keep track of in your inventory.

QuickBooks will not monitor quantities for these goods.
- **Items of service:** These are the services you provide to your customers. For example, gardening or accounting services.
- **Items that are not in stock:** These are goods you buy or sell but can't keep track of as inventory. For example, the nuts and bolts utilized in the installation process.
- **Bundles:** You may combine many products or services into one by using bundles. For example, a gift basket filled with cheese, wine, or fruit. You may avoid choosing each item separately on invoices or receipts by grouping items together.

Once everything is set up, you keep track of the items in your inventory as they sell. To keep an eye on your sales:
- Make an invoice if payment is due later
- Provide a sales receipt if your customer paid you immediately away.
- Learn how to submit an application for QuickBooks Payments.

QuickBooks then deducts the amount on the sales receipt or invoice from the amount that is now available. Keep an eye on what's in stock and what has to be ordered while working on an invoice, sales receipt, or other kind of transaction. Just slide your pointer over the amount you entered for an item to get additional details. If you have set reorder points, QuickBooks will also alert you when something is running short. If you have a low stock alert set up, QuickBooks will warn you when something is running short. QuickBooks alerts you when it's time to restock. QuickBooks allows for the direct ordering of inventory. Note what you purchase from vendors and what you still have on order. As a result, the amount on hand automatically rises as you get more items.

Automating purchase orders and inventory adjustments

Inventory Automation

Distributors, wholesalers, and retailers have started automating more inventory management processes across all sectors. Automation may reduce the time and effort required to execute repetitive operational activities. Businesses may efficiently grow operations and streamline inventory processes using today's technologies. By putting in place an automated inventory management system, businesses can streamline operations, monitor every link in their supply chain, and expand rapidly. Automated inventory management is the use of software technology to reduce the number of human labor-intensive tasks associated with product transportation and stocking. There are several advantages to automating inventory management. Among the most common applications are real-time inventory counts, location tracking, purchase orders, and reorder point automation.

The advantages of inventory automation for your company

Inventory automation and supply chain management turn out to be quite beneficial. A recent McKinsey study of consumer packaged goods (CPG) companies found that an automated supply chain may reduce supply chain costs by 10%, reduce excess inventory by 20%, and increase revenue by up to 4%. **These are the primary ways that automated inventory management systems may enhance the operations of your business.**

- **Enhanced data accuracy:** One of the purported benefits of computerized inventory management is increased accuracy. With all of the moves required for inventory and warehouse management, teams may quickly get fatigued. Data input and other time-consuming human work are significantly reduced by automation. Furthermore, conventional techniques can only provide rough approximations, especially during the time between stock counts; inventory management software, on the other hand, continually logs and monitors all aspects, including purchase orders and available stock levels. Automation allows businesses to handle hundreds of transactions daily, reduces the likelihood of human mistake, and improves inventory management by using accurate, current data.

- **Optimized resources:** Several routine tasks are involved in warehouse and inventory management. For instance, every time a product is received, sold, delivered, or returned, inventory levels must be updated and sent to the appropriate departments. It would be quite difficult for teams to do this task by hand. An automated system may be set up to swiftly do any number of tasks without requiring extra resources. By removing the need for teams to spend their time on repetitive and tiresome activities, they can now work more swiftly and effectively. Additionally, this allows them to focus on more crucial matters.

+ **Lower costs:** Accuracy and efficiency improvements are complemented by lower overall costs. For example, controlling inventory levels may save a lot of money by ensuring that a business only purchases items that it is likely to sell and prevents overstocking. Automating inventory management may assist determine how much stock needs to be purchased for the next sales cycle by collecting metrics like inventory turnover and sales estimates more consistently? This optimizes cash flow, minimizes physical work, and cuts shipping and storage costs.

Automated solutions are increasingly being employed in many aspects of business, from inputting customer data into Excel spreadsheets to monitoring orders through fulfillment. **Here are a few examples of inventory automation in action.**

+ **Consumer order entries:** Manufacturers and retailers often need a lot of resources to input and monitor consumer orders. Overstretched resources and potential operational bottlenecks during peak seasons or other demand fluctuations might arise from this attempt. To manage the burden, some could even choose to hire more people. Inventory automation for order input and modifications allows businesses to grow up to accommodate additional orders while effectively saving time.

+ **Warehouse and inventory management:** Inventory storage facilities handle thousands of parts, not simply product SKUs. This includes logistics-related goods, machinery, equipment, and packaging. Traditional warehouse operations involve all storage and logistical duties being completed by hand, which becomes unmanageable when facilities and inventory quantities rise. Automated systems can trace every product that passes through the warehouse and aggregate data on a single platform. Mobile barcode scanning and point-of-sale (POS) systems are two examples of these technologies.

+ **Fulfillment of customer orders:** Automation may be used to monitor customer orders in addition to inventory products being tracked from supplier to warehouse. Real-time inventory levels may be used to update product availability on e-commerce sites so that consumers can only order what is presently in stock, as well as assist companies in deciding whether to restock items based on sales data. Automation may also be utilized to notify customers about their orders at every delivery step. By keeping consumers and companies informed about the purchase process, this attention to detail raises overall customer satisfaction.

Tools for Forecasting and Budgeting

The expansion of any business is contingent upon optimizing performance and accomplishing strategic objectives. Budgeting and forecasting are two crucial processes in this case. Budgeting and forecasting are two crucial financial management strategies used by companies for long-term planning. Both are necessary for making educated decisions, setting realistic financial goals, and tracking progress toward those targets.

Making a budget

You may ensure that your financial resources and activities align with your overall strategy and objectives by creating a budget. It helps you plan, organize, communicate, regulate, and evaluate performance in order to achieve your company's goals and objectives. The process involves calculating cash flows, production lines, working capital, capital expenditures, sales, and costs over a certain period of time. You may compare the budgeted outcomes for actuals with expected results to identify any differences or areas for improvement.

The Forecasting

By using analytical tools, market circumstances, trends, and historical data, the forecasting approach makes predictions about your company's future performance.
Forecasting helps you:
- Identify the possible market for your products.
- Plan your production and inventory levels.
- Put money and resources aside.
- Set goals and strategies for action, and

Examine performance and potential hazards

Forecasting may be done for short-, medium-, or long-term periods, depending on your company's requirements. Depending on the reliability and accessibility of the data, forecasting may be done using both qualitative and quantitative methods.

Making financial estimates and budgets

Making financial plans

Organizations often utilize budgets as a way to manage their money. Create a budget for the next quarter, month, or year after assessing your assets and liabilities. With

QuickBooks, you can use all of your financial information to create the balance sheet or profit and loss budgets that your company needs. This gives you a summary to help you compare your actual income and spending with your budget. To establish a new budget, you must log in as an administrator or as a user who has the required rights. Additionally, administrators who have access to just budgets may establish special roles. This is the approach.

Examine the business's fiscal year

Check that the fiscal year start date in QuickBooks is correct. While you may begin creating a budget at any time throughout the fiscal year, it is more advantageous to do so.

- Navigate to Settings ☐ to choose Account and Settings.
- Select the tab for Advanced.
- Examine the Accounting section's field for the first month of the fiscal year. Select Edit if it's incorrect.
- Click Save after selecting the required month from the dropdown menu.

Make a budget

To create a budget, you may use your past financial data or previous budgets in QuickBooks. If this is your first budget, start here. You may even decide to clone one after you've set your first budget. Spreadsheet Sync may also be used to import an Excel file or create a budget straight from Excel. **Note:** QuickBooks Online creates the budget accounts list based on your chart of accounts. Make any necessary additions to your chart of accounts before drafting the budget.

- Select Budgeting by going to Settings.

- Make the decision to create a budget.

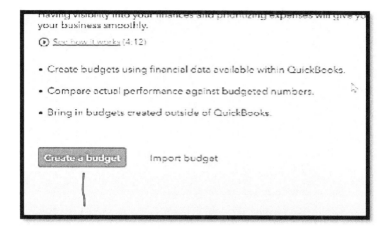

Make a budget for profits and losses

- Select Budgeting by going to Settings.
- Select the option "Create Budget."
- Select the kind of budget for profit and loss.

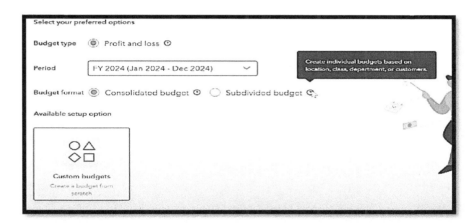

- Select the fiscal year for which the budget is being prepared.
- Choose the budget's format: Budgets may be split up or merged.
  - ➢ Decide whatever criteria, like class or geography, you want to utilize to divide the funds.

Make a unique budget

- Select Budgeting by going to Settings.
- Select the existing budget that you want to change.
- To modify the budget title, click Edit ✎ next to the automatically created title.

110

- If you want to utilize historical actual or historical budget data as a guide, turn on the Compare reference data toggle and choose the kind of reference data you want to use.
- If you want to preload your budget with the reference data, click the box next to Accounts. This will allow you to choose certain rows or all of the rows. Click on Batch operations and choose Copy reference data.
- Now enter your budget for every account. Using the settings icon in the top right corner, you may choose between the Yearly, Quarterly, and Monthly views, depending on the kind of budget you need.
- Select Save or Save and close.

Modify a budget

- In QuickBooks, make any required changes to a budget:
- Select Budgeting after navigating to Settings.
- Examine the list to determine your spending limit.
- Select View/modify from the Options menu to view or modify.
- Change each account one month at a time.
- To change the timeframe from monthly to quarterly or annual, choose one of the Yearly, Quarterly, or Monthly views.
- Select Save or Save and close.

Run reports on the budget

You may create personalized profit and loss budget reports to help you remain on top of your financial goals.

- Go to Settings and choose Budgeting.
- Examine the list to determine your spending limit
- In the Options column, choose the ▼menu. Next, click on Run Budget Overview or Run Budgets vs. Actuals.
- Use the reports export option to export a budget in Excel or PDF format.

Comparing performance to budgets

Any business has to maintain its budgets, and QuickBooks users would agree that identifying budget deviations is an essential part of financial management. This part covers the budget variance formula, report selection methods, dollar and percentage variance calculation, results analysis, and recording of insightful comments for remedial actions that result in higher profitability. The budget variance is the difference between your expected or projected revenue and spending and the actual results. You may evaluate the effectiveness of your budget and spot issues that might improve your financial planning and decision-making by monitoring variances. In accounting, the budget variance is the difference between the budgeted amount and the actual amount for a financial account over time. Actual performance exceeds the budget when there is a positive variance and falls short when there is a negative variance. You may use QuickBooks to calculate budget variance for any revenue or spending account to explain deviations from your objectives. This facilitates the assessment of the budget's accuracy and effectiveness. The budget variance is the gap between actual and anticipated income and costs. This makes it easy to compare financial performance to expectations.

To see a difference in the QuickBooks budget:

- Navigate to Reports > Budget vs. Actuals under Forecasts & Budgets.
- Choose the time period to look at.
- Analyze the variations for each account.

The report looks at the difference between planned and actual performance throughout the selected period. Positive variances indicate that actual performance surpassed budgets, whilst negative variances imply overspending.

Key things to discuss in the report:

- The total deviation in the company's budget helps assess overall performance.
- **Some account deviations:** Points out specific areas where performance is either too high or too low.
- **Revenue and cost variances:** Analyzes how well sales and expenses align with forecasts.
- **Largest budget variations:** View the biggest deltas for further analysis with ease.

By examining past budget deviations, financial strategies are enhanced and future projections are directed. Commentary provides the business context to stakeholders who comprehend the numbers. Comparing your planned amounts to actual data is necessary to track the financial performance of your business. The Budget vs. Actual report in QuickBooks Online makes this simple.

In order to generate this report:

- After signing in, go to the Reports area of your QuickBooks Online account.
- From the Business Overview category, choose the "Budget vs. Actual" report.
- From the drop-down option at the top, choose the budget to compare against.

The following figures will be shown in the report's columns:

- The sums allotted during the time frame
- Actual amounts set aside for that period of time
- What distinguishes the two

By looking at variances, you may identify situations where actual spending differs greatly from the budget. This might stimulate further investigation into the causes of the differences. For example, if your monthly ad expenditure was $1,500 above budget, look at the transactions to see whether the increase was due to a single campaign or a general pattern in ad spending. Determining if future budget changes are necessary may be aided by this knowledge. The typical Budget vs. Actual report may be improved by creating custom reports that compare other balances, such revenue or payroll. The flexibility of QuickBooks' reporting makes it simple to compare each month's budget with reality.

Practice Exercises

- Utilize QuickBooks Online to automate company procedures.
- Create recurring purchases.
- Set up payroll functions.
- Payroll processing and its advantages.
- Control the amount of inventory.
- Automate purchase orders and inventory adjustments.
- Make financial plans.

CHAPTER FIVE

PRIVACY AND DATA SECURITY IN QUICKBOOKS ONLINE 2025

The Value of Cloud-Based Solutions' Data Security

Businesses are creating, collecting, and storing massive amounts of data every second in the big data age we are living in. This data may include less sensitive information like marketing and behavioral analytics, as well as highly sensitive commercial or personal customer data. Cloud services are being used by businesses to enable increasingly remote or hybrid workforces, boost agility, and reduce time to market, in addition to the growing volumes of data that companies need to be able to access, manage, and analyze. Security teams are finding that they must reevaluate both their current and past approaches in order to safeguard cloud data as the traditional network barrier rapidly disappears. Data and applications are located outside of data centers, and more individuals than ever work remotely. Businesses must thus choose how to protect data and manage access to it as it moves across different contexts.

Cloud data security best practices are based on the same core principles as information security and data governance:

- **Data confidentiality:** Only processes or people with permission may access or change data. In other words, you need to ensure that your company's data is kept private.
- The dependability, validity, and trustworthiness of data are referred to as data integrity. In this case, it is essential to implement rules or processes to prevent data loss or tampering.
- **Data availability:** Data must be available and accessible to authorized users and processes when required, even if you want to prohibit unauthorized access. You'll need to ensure consistent uptime and keep systems, networks, and devices functioning correctly.

Recognizing the importance of safeguarding financial information

The epidemic's rapid changes in online use created a perfect atmosphere for hackers to thrive. Despite a sharp rise in cyberattacks in recent years, the banking sector seems to be the most susceptible. Cybercriminals were on the rampage, targeting financial services with ransomware attacks, bank account theft, and other crimes. By 2022, cyberattacks on financial services firms had grown by 257%. Thieves often target banks and other financial organizations in an attempt to get critical information that they can then sell on the dark web. These changes highlight the need for improved data security and privacy in the banking industry. Financial industry participants are increasingly using specialist financial software to bolster their cybersecurity efforts. Because of these systems' superior security features, bankers can easily protect themselves from hackers.

Data Protection Is legally required

Safeguarding personal information not only gives your business a competitive advantage but also ensures its existence. All companies that handle or process financial data are obligated by law to keep it safe, secure, and out of the hands of roaming hackers. Financial institutions must abide by a number of strict rules. These consist of the Payment Card Industry Data Security Standard (PCI DSS) (HIPAA), the General Data Protection Regulation (GDPR), and the Health Insurance Portability and Accountability Act. To adhere to these regulations and protect sensitive personal information, financial service providers must use robust security measures. Data security and privacy in the financial industry include more than simply the use of encryption, firewalls, and access restrictions. A robust organizational structure with integrated reporting procedures is required for cybersecurity operations. Customized financial software helps create a safe network that conforms to all industry regulations. It also helps to develop a culture of cybersecurity awareness in the workplace.

Adapts to Changing Cyberattacks

Cybercriminals diligently monitor computer networks for weeks or months, looking for weaknesses and vulnerabilities. By upgrading to more sophisticated networks, financial service companies are making their systems impenetrable. Cybercriminals are compelled to modify their tactics in order to capitalize on human mistake. Hackers usually target workers in the financial services sector with malware and phishing techniques. Workers give hackers access to the network when they inadvertently download malware or click on a phishing email. Hackers will install malware on your machine and take trade secrets and other valuable information. Even worse, they may take over your system and target your customers with phishing emails in order to obtain their login credentials. They often steal your customers' identities or swindle them of their money.

Decrease in Financial Losses

The financial sector bears the highest costs of cybercrime. A data breach in the banking industry typically costs $5.97 million, which is a huge sum. The cost may increase if a data breach leads to a ransomware assault. Hackers that target sensitive transactional data include sophisticated persistent threats, malware, phishing, DDoS attacks, and data exfiltration. It is used by cybercriminals to take over transactional systems and steal user account data in order to steal money or disrupt operations. The costs of data breaches are exorbitant since they include both direct and indirect expenses. Demands for ransom may vary from hundreds to millions of dollars, and ransomware attacks often lead to significant expenses. Hackers often indicate the ransom demand as a percentage of the company's annual sales. However, experts think that the direct effects of a data breach might only account for a very small portion of the overall costs. Indirect costs from data breaches are much higher. Between the ensuing downtime, data recovery, and virus eradication, the costs may add up. It typically takes a business 22 days to fully recover from a ransomware attack.

Prevents harm to one's reputation

Reputational damage is virtually always the result of a financial institution's data leak. The resulting damage might be costly if social media users or media outlets discover the vulnerability. Significant damage to a financial service company's reputation might lead to further losses. It's likely that you'll lose a lot of existing customers and have trouble attracting new ones. Restoring a damaged brand image after a data breach may be challenging and time-consuming. You will probably face severe penalties from the regulating agency in addition to the ransom paid and the increasing indirect costs. Being hacked is seen as a breach of contract, and government monitoring agencies impose severe penalties for such violations.

An overview of the security features of QuickBooks Online

Data security is now the top worry for businesses of all sizes. When managing financial data, it is essential to guarantee its integrity and protection. Many organizations use QuickBooks Online because of its ease of use and accessibility. But how safe is the online storage of your data? Even though you've likely heard a lot about the advantages that QuickBooks Online provides businesses, you may still be wondering, "Is my data secure in QuickBooks?"

This section provides the answer.

- **Encryption:** QuickBooks Online ensures the security of your data by encrypting it both during transmission and storage on Intuit's servers. By making your data unintelligible, encryption prevents unwanted users from accessing it.

- In addition to passwords, QuickBooks Online offers Multi-Factor Authentication (MFA) as an additional security feature. MFA requires users to provide two or more verification factors, such a password and a unique code delivered to a registered device, before granting access. Even in the event that login credentials are taken, this significantly reduces the possibility of unauthorized access.

- **Regular Data Backups:** QuickBooks Online data is routinely backed up by Intuit to prevent data loss in the case of system outages, natural disasters, or cyberattacks. These backups lessen the chance of downtime and the loss of crucial data by ensuring that your data can be restored to a specific point in time.

- **Safe Data Centers:** Intuit-managed data centers that adhere to strict physical security procedures, such as surveillance, access restrictions, and environmental controls, are where QuickBooks Online data is kept safe. Your data is protected by these measures against theft, loss, and unauthorized physical access.

- **Data Redundancy:** QuickBooks Online employs data redundancy across several servers and regions to provide high availability and fault tolerance. In the event of a server failure or outage, your data is automatically transferred to a different server, reducing disruptions and ensuring uninterrupted access.

- **User Permissions:** QuickBooks Online allows you to control who may access your data by assigning roles and permissions to users. You may reduce the likelihood of unauthorized modifications or data breaches by restricting access to certain features, transactions, or reports based on the duties of users in your organization.

- **Activity Logs:** QuickBooks Online maintains comprehensive logs of all user actions inside the system, including account settings modifications, data revisions, and logins. Because they show who accessed your data and what modifications were done, these logs aid in security audits and investigations.

- QuickBooks Online enables safe file transmission for documents and attachments by encrypting data during upload, download, and storage. This ensures that confidential documents, including as invoices, receipts, and financial statements, are protected while being sent.

- **Compliance Certifications:** QuickBooks Online complies with SOC 2, HIPAA, GDPR, and other industry standards and legislation. These certifications demonstrate Intuit's commitment to maintaining stringent security protocols and shielding your data from abuse, disclosure, and illegal access.

- **Secure connectivity with Third-Party Apps:** QuickBooks Online offers secure connectivity with third-party apps via the Intuit Developer Platform. Because these integrations follow Intuit's security requirements and undergo rigorous security audits, your data is safe as it travels across applications.
- **Data Exporting Options:** QuickBooks Online offers you total control over your data and the opportunity to backup it for further security. Your data may be exported whenever you want. You may export your data and ensure compatibility with other accounting programs or systems by using standard export formats like CSV or Excel.
- **Continuous Monitoring and Threat Detection:** Intuit employs state-of-the-art monitoring and threat detection technologies to identify and address security threats immediately. These technologies alert security staff to any possible dangers or anomalies that might indicate a security breach by monitoring user behavior, system activity, and network traffic.

Putting Security Measures in Place

Configuring role-based access and user permissions

You will learn how to create and manage custom roles for QuickBooks Online Advanced users in this section. **Be aware:**
- Only administrators and custom users with user management permissions are able to manage users. Learn how to assume the role of primary administrator.
- Some read-only fields are automatically provided in a role for your information.
- By establishing custom roles that only provide users the access necessary for their particular position; you may manage user access in QuickBooks. Choose which QuickBooks features users may access and interact with, including banking, sales, payroll, spending, reports, budgeting, and inventory.

When you create a new position, you have the option to:
- Create a new role and provide it access to certain resources.
- Choose a pre-made, personalized position (e.g., Sales Manager, Expense Manager).
- Choose a QuickBooks position from the list, such as company admin or time tracking only.

Include a new position

To create a new custom role, you just need to add it and choose which places it may access.
- Go to Settings ⚙ and choose Manage Users.

- Select the Roles tab, then select Add role.
- Enter the name and description of the position.
- Click Save Role after you've selected what the QuickBooks user role may access.
- Give a new user a role.
- Any new users you add to QuickBooks need to have a role assigned to them.
- After selecting Settings ⬚, choose Manage Users.
- Click on Add User after selecting the Users tab.
- Enter the user's initial name, last name, and email address here.
- From the Roles menu's ▼ dropdown, choose the role you want to assign to the user.
- Click Send invitation after reviewing the permissions allocated to this position.
- The user has to choose Let's Go! to log in after an invitation by email.

Footnote: If your user forgets their password, they may choose to reset it.

Give a new user a unique role

If you have particular responsibilities for new users, you must assign these to them and add them to QuickBooks.
- Go to Settings ⬚ and choose Manage Users.
- Click on Add User after selecting the Users tab.
- Enter the user's initial name, last name, and email address here.
- In the Roles section, choose View all rights, and then grant the user the specific permissions you want them to have.
- Click Send invitation after the permissions have been checked.
- You will be required to establish a new role since you have used custom permissions.
- Enter the custom role name and role description here.
- Select the option "Save the role."

Let's Go must be selected by the user! To log in after an invitation by email.

Modify a user role

There can be times when you need to provide a user more access or when their job changes. This is how a user's role may be changed.
- After selecting Settings ⬚, choose Manage Users.
- Locate the user you want to change by selecting the Users tab.
- Select Edit from the Action column.
- Choose either the existing custom roles or the QuickBooks roles.

- Click "Save." If you choose a role and then alter permissions, you will be asked to save a new custom role. Click Save Role after the role has been named and described.

Personalized roles and access

Using custom roles, you may give certain QuickBooks sections particular access by defining:
- Which features are accessible to QuickBooks users?
- What is possible with certain features, including see only, create, edit, delete, approve, and full access
- Which data limitations apply to their access, such as location-based limitations on sales data?

Setting up password regulations and two-factor authentication

Two-factor authentication (2FA) is a security method for identity and access management that requires two distinct forms of identification in order to provide access to data and resources. With the use of 2FA, businesses can keep an eye on and help safeguard their most critical networks and data. 2FA is used by employers to protect their employees' personal and business assets. Because it prevents hackers from accessing, stealing, or deleting your internal data records for their own benefit, this is crucial. The advantages of adopting 2FA are many. For example, 2FA users are not required to download or carry an app that is linked to a token generator. The majority of websites employ a customized 2FA, text message, or phone call to verify your identity on your mobile device.

Additional advantages of 2FA include:
- It is not required to use a hardware token generator. These types of 2FA codes are often lost or forgotten. However, 2FA procedures are now much more useful due to contemporary technologies.
- Password generators are more efficient than traditional passwords. Generators are the safest option since no two passcodes are the same.
- Maximum passcode input prevents hackers from breaking in and accessing private information.
- The process is simple to comprehend and manage.

You have the option to voluntarily activate two-step verification for your Intuit account. If enabled, we will use a one-time passcode to verify your identity each time you log in on any device. Changing the phone number linked to your Intuit Account will immediately disable two-step verification. But you may use your new number to turn it back on.

To activate two-step verification, do the actions listed below:
- Log in to your Intuit account.
- Select Security and log in.
- In the "2-step verification" section, choose Turn on.
- Select the setup.
- Before selecting the method you want to use to confirm your account, make sure your phone number is correct:
  - **Text message:** You get a standard six-digit verification text code.
  - **Voice message:** You get an automated voice verification code in English.
- Click "Continue."
- Click Proceed after you have entered the code we emailed you.
- Once your account password has been entered, click "Continue."
- Two-step verification has started, according to a message. Select Close to finish. You will also get an email confirming that your security choices have been updated.

After you've activated two-step verification, you may use your preferred authenticator app to create your verification codes. **To get started, follow these steps:**
- To get an authenticator app, search for "authenticator" on Google Play or the iOS App Store.
- Log in to your Intuit account.
- Select Security and log in.
- Select an authenticator.
- To install the Authenticator app, click on it.
- Follow the on-screen instructions to complete the setup procedure.

You could be asked to complete two-step verification for a number of reasons, such as the kind of device, network, or browser you use to access Intuit products. If we are unable to establish a sufficient feeling of confidence based on these reasons, you may be asked to verify yourself in order to make sure that your account has not been hacked. Because of third-party software, such as an ad blocker, you may still need to verify yourself even if you are certain that the device you are using to log in is trustworthy. In this case, you need either add the *.intuit.com domain to the list of domains that your ad blocker permits or deactivate it expressly for the *.intuit.com domain.

Strategies for routine data backup and recovery

More than 29 million small businesses in the US use QuickBooks Online as their primary accounting software. Nearly every organization favors it due to its user-friendly UI and many connections. The Shared Responsibility Model backup approach is used by

QuickBooks Online, however many SaaS systems do not provide the recovery of particular account data from backups. Accounting companies use QuickBooks Online to handle a number of customers, while SMBs use it for routine bookkeeping and accounting. QuickBooks Online creates platform-wide backups; however these backups are not able to recover particular account data, such as transactions, expenses, and reports. If any of that information were lost or hacked, reconstructing the data would be very stressful and challenging. Additionally, it would be difficult to convince customers to entrust you with their accounts. For many financial professionals, backups of their financial data are essential rather than optional. Regulators are paying more attention to accountants and bookkeepers because hackers are increasingly targeting the banking sector and related businesses. Companies must also comply with a growing number of regulations, including the FTC Safeguards, NY Shield, GDPR, and IRS 4557. Legally, cloud accounting systems that store and handle financial data—particularly personally identifiable information, or PII—must now have robust security safeguards in place. This isn't just a convenience anymore. Systems for backing up financial data online can help companies stay audit-ready. Companies are required by a number of regulations, including SOC, to show auditors that they routinely backup sensitive client data and are able to restore it quickly in the case of data loss or corruption. Audit logs that specify the when and by whom of backups and restorations help to accelerate and ease compliance with different requirements. Make a backup of your company so you always have a copy of your chart of accounts. Unwanted changes made to settings, customers, suppliers, and other data may also be undone if needed. This is the approach. **You must first determine which data you can and cannot support. Here are some statistics you can support:**

- Invoices
- Estimates
- Sales
- Receipts
- Payments
- Deposits
- Bills and bill payments
- Credit memos
- Vendor credits
- Journal entries
- Purchases and purchase orders
- Refund receipts
- Time activities
- Transfers
- Accounts
- Budgets
- Classes
- Currencies

- Customers
- Departments
- Employees (except their SSN)
- Items
- Payment methods
- Tax agencies
- Tax codes and tax rates
- Terms
- Vendors (except the Tax fields)
- Attachments
- Company Info
- Entitlements
- Exchange rates
- Preferences
- Intuit Payroll info backs up as journal entries
- Inventory shrinkage and adjustments back up as journal entries

The following data cannot be backed up:

- Details about QuickBooks Online Payments
- Types of customers and pricing guidelines
- Credits and charges that are delayed (even though related invoices are supported)
- recurring deals
- Bank feeds and the connections they have to transactions and policies
- reports for reconciliation
- Billable expenses depending on accounts
- Billable expenses based on items with a markup
- personalized reports
- Personal form designs
- Entries in the audit log

Everything may be restored from a backup, with the exception of:

- Budgets need to be exported as CSV files.
- Inventory does not include inventory history or modifications.
- The Online Backup and Restore application restores tax rates from your spending accounts to your liability accounts.
- Your cloud account, like Dropbox or Google Drive, stores data in the.cab format once it has been locally backed up using the Local Backup option. At this time, recovering data from a local backup is not supported.

QuickBooks will automatically backup your data when you use the Online Backup and Restore feature. After it is finished, it will monitor any changes made to the data of your business. A backup from any time may then be restored.

- Go to the Settings [].

- ✦ Choose the backup business.
- ✦ Please be aware that before choosing Authorize, you may need to log into your Intuit account.

Use these procedures to manually build a one-time backup:

Maybe you want to save everything while working on a big project. Not a problem. Manual backups are always possible. **Here's how.**

- ✦ Go to Settings ⬚ and
- ✦ Choose the backup provider. **Reminder:** Before choosing Authorize, you may need to log into your Intuit account.
- ✦ Choose "Add Company."

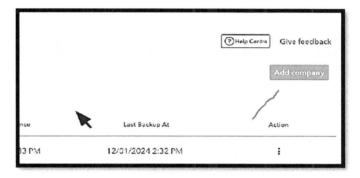

- ✦ To support a business, choose the relevant company from the "Search for a company" dropdown option.

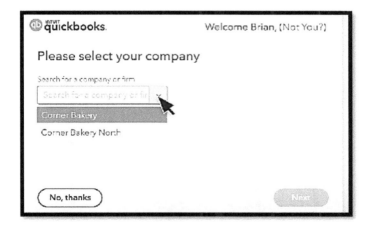

- ✦ Select Next, followed by Connect. Note: Repeat steps 2–4 if you have many organizations to support.
- ✦ Find the company you want to support.

- Click on Action ▼ and choose Run complete backup.

Backups may be saved to Google Drive after your accounts are linked. To set everything up, follow these steps.

- Go to the Settings ▢ .
- Choose the backup business. Note: Before choosing Authorize, you may need to log into your Intuit account.
- Select the User option.
- Choose the location where you want to save your backup. Select Google Drive Link.
- Follow the instructions to allow QuickBooks to create backups.
- The file may not appear in Google Drive for ten minutes or more. Additionally, at this time, Online Backup and recovery cannot be used to recover data saved using Local Backup.

Bring your data back from a backup

To retrieve data from a certain date and time, use the backup. Although it is often significantly faster, restoring a backup may take up to an hour. The business operates more quickly the less data it has. Important: While the Online Backup and Restore application recovers your data, do nothing else in your company. A checkmark will appear on the status after it is finished. At that point, it's safe to come back and work for your organization.

- Go to Settings, and then choose Backup Business. Note: After checking in with your Intuit account, you may need to select Authorize in order to proceed.
- Find the company whose image you want to restore.
- From the Action ▼ dropdown menu, choose Restore.

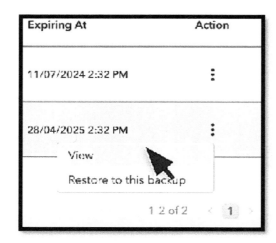

- From the Date field, choose the date you want to restore, and from the Time ▼ dropdown menu, select the time you want to restore.

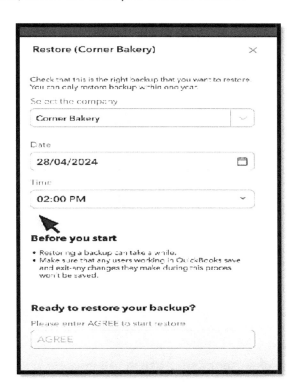

- Press Next. Follow the instructions given.
- Select the option "Start Restore."

Adherence to Rules and Guidelines

Recognizing the prerequisites for compliance

To operate lawfully, businesses must follow rules governing their safety procedures, labor practices, and commercial dealings. Before launching your company, you should be informed of the laws that apply to your sector and maintain a log of all the costs and due dates involved in adhering to those requirements. Internal and external compliance rules are the two categories. For certain commercial entities (such corporations, LLCs, etc.), state governments often need internal compliance procedures. Senior staff members of the firm create and carry out these policies internally. External compliance refers to rules that are enforced and imposed by a federal or state entity.

Internal needs for doing business

The strict internal requirements that companies must follow include establishing a board of directors, conducting annual and inaugural director meetings, creating and updating bylaws, allocating stock to shareholders, and documenting all stock transactions. It is highly advised that LLCs and other small businesses keep accurate and current records of all company transactions, as well as any relevant changes to standards or operations, even if they are not subject to the same restrictions as corporations. Document templates and compliance kits, which may contain operating agreements, stock certificates, seals, and example meeting minutes in addition to sample bylaws, may help you organize and satisfy your internal compliance requirements. Internal standards are primarily intended to ensure that a business is run honestly and free from corruption and other corrupting influences. Regulations pertaining to external compliance will also apply to certain parts of the business, such stock sales.

Needs of the external government

The external criteria for companies are approved by the states where you are incorporated and where you do business. **The following are examples of common external needs:**

+ Every year, a report or statement is released. Many states require corporations and LLCs to submit annual reports in order to retain accurate data on these entities. A biannual statement could also be required by certain states. There is often a fee associated with submitting a statement or report, which may vary from $10 to over $300.
+ The franchise tax. Some states may require corporations or limited liability companies to pay a franchise tax in order to operate. The amount is determined using calculations based on a number of variables, such as the number of shares issued at par value by a company or the yearly income generated, and is established by the state that collects it.
+ A law pertaining to fair labor standards. All businesses, including LLCs, are required to abide by the Fair Labor Standards Act (FLSA). The Fair Labor Standards Act (FLSA) establishes minimum wages, overtime pay, and recordkeeping obligations for both full-time and part-time workers in the United States. Because FLSA rules differ from state to state, company owners must be aware of them and take the necessary steps to comply.

Because deadlines and report costs vary from state to state be sure you are aware of the rules in the states where you want to do business. Note that several jurisdictions, like

California and Nevada, demand the filing of an initial report for a charge within a few months after formation.

Penalties and Repercussions for Non-Compliance

Since internal criteria are intended to ensure the most effective and ethical operation of a company, the executive, management, and board staff members choose the appropriate sanctions for a given transgression. Recurring infractions are often punished with a range of warnings or probation, which is followed by termination. The state enforces penalties for breaking external rules, and they may range widely in intensity. Like the taxes and restrictions, the types of penalties and fines will vary from state to state. Generally speaking, failure to meet external criteria might be seen as "piercing the corporate veil" by a company. In the event that the business is sued, this eliminates the organization's limited liability protection and makes the owner or owners personally responsible for any losses and damages. A company should follow the guidelines and have "good standing." Failure to do so might result in a late charge or an interest payment deadline. If a business is administratively dissolved after not being in "good standing" for a long time, it may lose its LLC or corporation privileges. For example, in California, LLCs are required to provide an annual statement of information. Normally, it costs $25 to submit this statement. However, if the LLC does not file by the deadline, the Secretary of State's office may charge an additional $25 late fee each day, up to a maximum of $1,500. The business may eventually be shut down as a consequence of further noncompliance. When a business is suspended in California, it loses all legal authorization to operate as the kind of business entity it was intended to be and is unable to do so. Additionally, California state law voids contracts made by a suspended company.

Making sure QuickBooks Online conforms to industry norms

Over time, the format of financial reporting has evolved. Every country followed its own set of accounting guidelines when it came to financial reporting. There hasn't always been a formal list of internationally accepted accounting standards. Consequently, financial reports often lacked comprehensibility and acceptance. The goal of reporting in accounting is to make financial data measurable, recognizable, and presentable to stakeholders. Accountants are aware that there are several methods for reporting on the flow of funds inside an organization. To ensure that reports are readily understood by stakeholders, governments enforce adherence to certain requirements. Accounting standards are guidelines and practices for managing transactions. For individuals who are making financial choices, these financial accounts provide helpful information on cash flow, position, and performance. In today's worldwide corporate climate, comparable, transparent, and reliable reporting systems are essential for accurate financial information in order to assist businesses operating abroad and attract investors. This is the outcome of countries all across the globe agreeing on international norms. These principles are known as the International Financial Reporting Standards (IFRS). IFRS is used to standardize most accounting procedures worldwide. Standardizing reporting standards across different worldwide markets was the worldwide Accounting Standards Board's (IASB) goal. In order for investors and company owners to make educated financial choices, IFRS standards are designed to maintain financial transparency. The standards provide data credibility, comparability, and uniformity worldwide. This makes it easier for countries and businesses to analyze financial data. It allows report readers to compare things side by side, to put it another way. Providing more confidence to investors when they choose to invest in countries with open financial reporting laws.

The IFRS criteria are listed below:

Financial Position Statement

The balance sheet is another name for it. This guideline requires that companies' financial sheets be transparent. A company's financial health is reported and tracked by looking at its balance sheets after the accounting period, which include assets, owner equity, and liabilities.

Profit and loss statement

A revenue statement is another name for it. IFRS requires a single profit and loss statement. According to IAS 1, this is the primary financial statement used to evaluate a company's performance. This may be shown as a single statement of comprehensive income or as a combination of a profit and loss statement and a statement of comprehensive income. Even if IFRS has no predetermined structure, a number of things are required, such as revenue, financing expenses, tax charges, etc.

Statement of Equity Changes

Similar to the US GAAP retained earnings statement. By comparing equity across accounting periods, this report offers a more comprehensive view of the company's growth over the last 12 months.

Cash Flow Statement

According to IAS 7, a statement of cash flow must be an essential part of a business's basic financial statements. This report displays cash inflows and outflows. The cash flow statement should be used to classify operating, investment, and financing cash flow.

Compliance Notes

A summary of the accounting rules. By outlining data and demonstrating the company's accounting procedures, these comments provide further explanation on the previously stated reports. According to IAS 8, this is required. It might take a lot of time for accounting specialists to gather all the required data. Accounting software like QuickBooks Online may save you time by making it much simpler to locate the numbers required for these reports. It is essential as IFRS encourages openness and trust in international financial markets. Investor trust in publicly listed companies that list their shares on the global financial market is bolstered by it. It ensures that the standardized financial reporting that companies provide to investors can be trusted. Comparing and evaluating the financial outcomes of companies that operate globally is another use for it.

GAAP vs. IFRS

One of the nations that have not yet completely adopted IFRS is the United States of America, whose accounting system is known as Generally Accepted Accounting Policies (GAAP) or US GAAP internationally. The Securities and Exchange Commission (SEC) enforces US GAAP, which was created by the Financial Accounting Standards Board (FASB). The main difference between IFRS and GAAP is that the latter is principle-based and allows for more flexibility, whilst the former is rule-based, more rigid, and offers less room for interpretation.

The two accounting frameworks differ significantly in the following ways:

- GAAP is far more rigorous and comprehensive than IFRS. This is due to the fact that IFRS must take into consideration differences with global firms, whereas GAAP just concentrates on US peculiarities, giving them greater depth. The IFRS regulations are more flexible and ambiguous to accommodate the needs of multinational corporations.
- IFRS and GAAP reporting vary from one another. For instance, IFRS broadens the definition of revenue and allows companies to report revenue sooner. Compared to a balance sheet prepared using GAAP, one produced using this approach may have a higher revenue stream.

- Reporting expenses differs from those under IFRS. One example is the establishment of future reinvestment funds (Assets). These expenses fall under GAAP. IFRS allows you to capitalize them.
  - The inventory rules of the two systems vary.
  - Under GAAP, inventory reversals are prohibited. Under certain circumstances, IFRS allows it.
  - **Using GAAP, inventories may be reported in three different ways.**
    - The procedure is known as First In, First Out, or FIFO.
    - The method of weighted average cost
    - IFRS does not allow the Last In, First Out (LIFO) method.

Notably, US GAAP compliance with IFRS has not advanced rapidly, despite the SEC's indications of a shift in that direction. This suggests that companies operating in the US and other markets need to generate financial statements that meet distinct standards.

Taking responsible care of sensitive data

The two main tendencies that are now prevalent should not come as a surprise to you at this point. First, businesses are gathering and utilizing more data to improve their core products. Second, a growing number of compliance and regulatory standards are being released by both public and private entities. As these businesses realize that collecting and using data improves sales, efficiency, and other goals, authorities are prepared to look at how the data is being used. This is for the best, of course. Businesses need to be able to access and utilize data quickly in order to remain lucrative and productive, but they also need to ensure that the data is secure in order to protect everyone's right to privacy. A company's productivity is essentially destroyed if it begins to pay penalties for violating any of the many and growing state regulations pertaining to personal data, such as GDPR, HIPAA, PCI, and others. Good data governance requires businesses to preserve the security and integrity of their data while maintaining high productivity levels.

Define sensitive data

You cannot accomplish your objectives unless you first create the framework for doing so. Many organizations get enthused about employing new technology or establishing creative work practices, but they put off thinking about the organizational structure until later. Policy should come first in order to minimize liabilities and maximize results. The first step is to determine what information you deem sensitive. You must keep this list wide since it might be tough to incorporate every piece of information that can be regarded sensitive. One way is to make a list of things you know are sensitive, such system data, passwords, and user lists. The collected data, such as customer names, trade secrets, financial information, and so on, may then be used. By giving several specific instances and leaving the policy open-ended for data you could acquire in the future, you assume that a significant amount of the information your team collects is sensitive. In this fashion, the policy should aid in instructing your staff to practice critical thinking when presented with facts that may be unique or not expressly mentioned in your list, allowing them to make the best judgments. Additionally, data may be grouped into several categories. All personal data is important, but sensitive data, such as a Social Security number or credit card number, is worth more than, say, a marketing team's early draft of an ad. It's also a good idea to identify the types of data that workers should never touch. For instance, you could seek to dodge the regulatory scrutiny that comes with obtaining credit card data due of PCI restrictions. If this is the case, you should explicitly state in business policy that staff are not permitted to collect credit card data. Once the data is intentionally obtained, you are accountable for it, regardless of whether you as a company decided you wanted it or not.

Evaluation

Your organization is likely managing sensitive data at some point in the cycle, whether you are just starting to collect data and construct your system or you are maintaining a system and planning the next step of your technology roadmap. In any event, it is appropriate to undertake compliance and/or risk assessment often, maybe once a year, but the actual frequency will depend on your requirements. You will need to make improvements as you design and maintain a system that maintains sensitive data following best practices. Even if you feel you are doing everything properly, a comprehensive examination will bring out any areas in which you fell short. Additionally, assessment findings that highlight your shortcomings will provide you the insight you need to make the right decisions in the first place. Most businesses hire smart people who are experts in their sector, but they may not be responsible for PCI compliance, for instance. You cannot assume that the sensitive data controls you implement today will continue to be sufficient in the future since standards are susceptible to change and evolution. Additionally, assessments should be conducted in the case of a major issue, such as a system failure caused by a hardware malfunction, connection loss, power outage, or security incident that exposed you to unacceptable levels of risk of a data breach.

Keeping

Once sensitive data has been defined, you can start creating rules for where it may be located in your surroundings. Data storage is the initial stage in this process. Start by considering how you would want your data to be organized digitally when it is being kept at rest, regardless of the platform. Ideally, data should be rationally organized based on how sensitive they are. This will help you create access restrictions for staff members with limited access as well as security and risk management plans specifically suited for sensitive data. This should be used wherever the data is found, but if it isn't organized logically, you won't be able to handle it efficiently. Despite having excellent security systems, many businesses still face these types of problems. Particularly in these exceptional times, you will probably be storing your sensitive information on the cloud in some way. However, even if you are keeping data locally, you still need to take compliance regulations like HIPAA, PCI, GDPR, and others carefully. It is not enough to choose a cloud storage service that offers security guarantees. Establish the compliance requirements you must follow, and then make sure the vendors you are thinking about satisfy those requirements and that their solutions are safe. Many businesses provide excellent services, but sometimes they fall short for certain types of sensitive data. Although going into the specifics of what controls you will need is outside the scope of this blog, some important things to think about are multi-factor authentication, encryption in transit and at rest, redundancy and backup plans, data center certifications, location, and audit trail, among other areas where the storage of your private information may be incompliant or compromised. How much you spend in these technology solutions and whose suppliers you choose will depend on the value of the data.

Sophisticated encryption is essential when keeping medical information on a server you use, but it is not necessary when sending emails asking about our lunch plans. Assuming—possibly a big assumption—that you have put in place the right controls, the next step is to make sure your team is utilizing your storage environment effectively. This presents the concept of shadow IT. This is the situation in which end users decide to utilize technology that is not controlled or approved by the company. This is getting more widespread as more individuals work from home and use their devices. No system can manage sensitive data safely if it is not being utilized as intended. Businesses that properly deploy compliant technology solutions are far less likely to encounter a security problem involving sensitive data, despite the fact that the news is full with really alarming stories of malicious hackers and data breaches.

Distributing

There is no data in a vacuum. Organizations usually provide sensitive information to other parties for justifiable reasons. For example, your HR department collects private data from your employees and gives it to the government, payroll companies, and other entities. But imagine if your HR department chose to utilize that information and delivered some of it via regular mail in a transparent envelope. Instead, they delivered it in four different ways, depending on how they were feeling, and there was no way to track it. The worst part is that they could have just provided a criminal with personal information by disclosing the names and addresses of the people they shared it with without doing any due diligence. Before exchanging sensitive information in the normal course of business, you must put up technological and operational controls. Start with the procedure and processes to achieve this. Take technology out of the equation and concentrate only on the responsibilities of team members who divulge confidential information to other parties. After that, you may develop a workable procedure to which technical advancements can be introduced in the future. If you know what your team needs to do, you can select the right products to complete the core task. Any data being transferred to a third party must be encrypted while in transit. You should also implement identity verification mechanisms to make sure that whatever sensitive information you do provide to a third party reaches the right people. You should also consider endpoint monitoring and device management solutions to stop infected machines from handling sensitive data. Finally, there need to be fewer channels for sharing private information. Not all file-sharing or messaging services that meet sensitive data compliance standards and have the ability to encrypt data in transit need to be used. As you utilize more technology to exchange data, you will need to manage and protect additional tools, which raises the risk. Once your IT solutions are in place, ensure that your staff members use them and refrain from using unauthorized sharing choices.

Elimination and Destroying

As businesses gather ever-increasing volumes of data, they construct information vaults that hold the data they need for operations. But as businesses grow the repository, they also raise the potential of liability and data breaches, which might result in fines, audits, and other consequences. Additionally, because both employees and devices ultimately leave the organization, there is a potential that data may be disclosed. You must thus have efficient rules and processes in place to deal with the destruction and deletion of data. If a device's hard disk contains any sensitive information when it is at rest, it should be destroyed when it is retired from frequent usage. The destruction should be done by a company that follows the law and maintains documentation of its activities. Devices that do not retain sensitive data but may have previously come into touch with it should be returned to their factory settings before being sent for recycling or donation. The specific guidelines for deleting and removing data will vary based on your particular compliance needs. Additionally, when a user leaves your organization, ensure sure their credentials are updated or revoked to prevent them from accessing the data they were previously given. Although IT departments and service providers may respond to change management needs to protect the business from risk, they are usually not aware of workforce changes, making this an essential management responsibility.

Effort and receptivity

You must have the finest risk management for the expenditures you make in protecting your sensitive data since there will be limitations on what can be done for firms managing sensitive data of any kind. To handle sensitive data properly and lawfully, one must always pay close attention to details and never take anything for granted. Keep in mind that the only thing that is constant is change.

Addressing Data Breach and Security Risks

You just learned that your business had a data breach. If an insider stole customer information, hackers stole personal information from your firm server, or the information was accidentally posted on your website, you may be unsure of what to do next. What should you do and who should you call if you believe that someone may have disclosed your personal information? Continue reading to find out precisely what you must do and, if necessary, who to call.

Recognizing typical security risks and weaknesses

A network security threat is just that—a danger to your data systems and network. Any effort to access your data by breaking into your network is considered a network threat. There are many different types of network attacks, and each has a distinct goal. Some attacks, including distributed denial-of-service (DDoS) efforts, try to overload your network or servers with too many requests in an attempt to bring them down. Other threats to your data include malware and credential theft. Others, like malware, will enter your company's network and wait to collect information about it. **Although there are many different types of network security threats, they typically fall into four categories:**

External threats

External threats to your business might come from people, organizations, or even natural catastrophes that could cause major disruptions to your network. This is achieved by exploiting a defect, weakness, or data loss that significantly affects the cyber security of your network and company operations.

Internal dangers

These are dangers from malicious insiders, such as irate or poorly vetted employees who are now working for a different company. Unfortunately, many businesses often face internal dangers. A 2022 Cybersecurity Insiders poll found that 57% of businesses think insider events have become more common over the last 12 months.

Threats that are structured

Structured threats are attacks that are executed by knowledgeable cybercriminals with a defined goal in mind. This category includes, for example, state-sponsored attacks.

Unorganized assaults

Unstructured assaults are random and often executed by amateurs without a specific goal in mind. Network threats are always changing and growing, and they may take many different shapes. Most likely, you are already aware of the most common dangers. These include sophisticated persistent threats, SQL injection, ransomware, malware, phishing, and DDoS.

Here are some special methods for spotting threats and weaknesses:

- **Keep an eye on your network:** The most important first step in identifying vulnerabilities and threats is to ensure visibility. You may evaluate your defenses from the viewpoint of an attacker by being aware of the threats that are most likely to affect your business and the weaknesses in your network.
- **Employing threat intelligence:** What kind of assaults is being undertaken, and what dangers may your company encounter? You can protect your business from assaults before they happen by being aware of the danger environment.
- **Penetration testing:** When the chips fall, where do your defenses break? Which employee is most likely to open a suspicious email and click on a risky link? Since you can't know unless you try, penetration testing is the best way to test your defenses.
- **Control permissions:** By dividing your network and limiting access, you may avoid malicious insiders and data breaches by limiting which employees have access to which parts of the network.
- Employing a firewall is advised for both internal and external usage. Firewalls prevent unauthorized users from accessing your network. They also keep an eye on all network traffic.
- Keep an eye on your network at all times: Security has to be constantly monitored in order to be successful. Once your controls are in place, make sure they are

regularly reviewed and updated to identify any new threats or vulnerabilities that can compromise your network.

Actions to do in the event of a security incident or data leak

Numerous factors may cause or exacerbate data breaches, which can include different types of personal data and have a range of actual or prospective negative effects on individuals and businesses. As a result, there isn't a single effective method for dealing with a data breach. Each breach has to be addressed separately, taking into account the risks it presents and the most effective way to reduce or eliminate those risks.

Following a data breach, four crucial steps should be taken in general:

- **Step one:** Close the data breach to prevent further compromises of personal information.
- **Step two:** The processes involved in evaluating a data breach include gathering information, evaluating the risks, including the potential for damage to the affected parties, and, if practical, taking action to reduce any risk of harm.
- **Step three:** If required, notify the Commissioner and the individuals in issue. If the breach meets the criteria for a "eligible data breach" under the NDB plan, notification to the entity could be necessary.
- **Step four:** Analyze the incident and consider what can be done to prevent future breaches of this kind.

When possible, entities must take remedial action to mitigate the effect of the breach on affected individuals. If remedial action is effective in lowering the chance that people may experience serious injury, the NDB scheme notification requirements may not be relevant.

In general, companies should:

- Treat any known or suspected data breaches seriously and take prompt action to contain, assess, and fix the problem. Even apparently minor violations might have major repercussions when everything is taken into account.
- Complete the first three phases (notify, assess, and contain) as soon as possible or simultaneously. In certain cases, it could be desirable to notify others immediately, before the breach is evaluated or controlled.
- Choose your response according to each situation. Depending on the breach, certain processes could be merged, while some stages might not be necessary. Depending on the details of the breach, a business may sometimes take further steps.

It's crucial to use the lessons gained from a data breach event to enhance the organization's security and handling protocols for personal data and reduce the probability that it will occur again. It's also important to consider any previous data breaches that are similar to the current one, since they can indicate a structural issue with policies or procedures. Employees should get training on any changes to relevant policies and procedures that may be implemented after a review in order to ensure a timely response to a data breach.

Using QuickBooks help to address security concerns

Every aspect of QuickBooks' operations is embedded with security and privacy. They know how valuable your information is. You can't afford to take any chances with it. Here are some guidelines for protecting your account and your financial information:

General advice

- Maintain the privacy of your Intuit passwords.
- Make sure your password is hard to figure out. Combine numbers and uppercase letters.
- A firewall and virus protection should be installed on each computer you use to access Intuit products.
- Avoid installing software from unfamiliar individuals or organizations.

The operation of your bank link

If you link your bank account, QuickBooks will safely and automatically download your transactions. By using your bank's current data rather than manually entering transactions, you may save time. QuickBooks will continuously download your transactions to keep your accounts up to date. In order to establish a one-way connection with your bank, they want your online banking user ID and password. The connection and your bank's data are "read-only". In other words, although QuickBooks may "read" the data, it cannot process payments or get private information from your transactions. Only one channel of information transfer is possible: from your bank account to QuickBooks.

How QuickBooks protects your data

QuickBooks uses state-of-the-art, generally recognized security and virus protection to safeguard your financial data. This includes servers that are protected by firewalls, sign-ins that need a password, and the same encryption technology that the world's top institutions utilize.

The physical location of your data

QuickBooks is kept on systems that are managed by Intuit. These are in your home country in order to adhere to data residency regulations. Data is kept on the cloud platform Amazon Web Services (AWS). This shows that many levels of physical access, network, and storage security are in place to secure your data. Backups provide redundancy for these systems.

Practice Exercises

- What role does data security play?
- How important is it to safeguard financial information?
- Set up user authorization.
- Make an efficient data backup.
- Bring up significant compliance needs.
- How should private data be managed?
- Recognize typical security risks and weaknesses pertaining to financial information at your company or place of employment.

CHAPTER SIX

THE QUICKBOOKS ONLINE INTEGRATION WITH OTHER TOOLS

Comprehending Add-Ons and App Integrations

QuickBooks integration is the process of combining QuickBooks Online with other third-party applications or platforms. More applications might be added to the platform, improving accuracy and saving time, by eliminating the need for manual data input and simplifying data transfer. Two advantages of QuickBooks syncing with other programs are that it streamlines operations and keeps data up to date across platforms. By integrating data from many systems, integration reduces the likelihood of discrepancies and enhances reporting. You will discover more about QuickBooks Online integration and the degree to which QuickBooks integrates with applications like as Shopify, Zapier, and others in this area.

Examining third-party applications and available integrations

For QuickBooks® Online, there are several tools and add-ons that work in unison to automate data input, accounting, invoicing, procedures, and more. These straightforward QuickBooks interfaces help small and medium-sized businesses run more efficiently. QuickBooks Online Advanced customers benefit from our growing collection of best-in-class Premium Apps, which provide you access to all of your important financial data in one place. Thanks to these adaptable solutions, business owners no longer have to spend hours manually inputting data and statistics.

Instead, these connections boost productivity and become QuickBooks your company's and your own financial single source of truth. Because there are hundreds of alternatives available in the QuickBooks software Store, it may be challenging to choose the appropriate software or add-on for your company. We have put together our list of the best QuickBooks applications and add-ons to assist you and your business in growing. View our QuickBooks App Store's top programs, such as the QuickBooks Online Advanced suite of Premium programs, which streamlines accounting, payroll, bookkeeping, and other financial duties.

The programs listed below are easily synchronized with QuickBooks Online:

Bill.com

One of the top-rated applications that you can sync with QuickBooks is Bill.com. Bill.com provides you more financial control by allowing you to create customized processes and routing rules for easier and faster approvals from any device. Using the Bill.com interface, your bank account information is synchronized with QuickBooks to help you manage your accounts payable and receivable. If you connect Bill.com to your QuickBooks Online Advanced account, you allow the deep linkage between bills in both systems, which is only possible via the Premium App. You may synchronize your book balance, accounts, invoices, suppliers, and customers with Bill.com and QuickBooks. This feature allows you to automate approval procedures, schedule payments, issue reminders, and more. You can easily access any bills that need to be paid using the Bill.com app.

HubSpot

If you need customer relationship management (CRM) software, the HubSpot connection is a must. By integrating HubSpot with QuickBooks, you can see all of your lead and customer data in one place. HubSpot is one of the best QuickBooks integrations, allowing businesses to integrate their accounting and CRM systems to reduce sales cycles and enhance communication between the finance and sales divisions. With QuickBooks Online Advanced and its HubSpot connectivity, customers may input draft invoices into QuickBooks. Additionally, they may design their own automated process to transfer invoices between HubSpot and Advanced from draft to review and approval.

Salesforce

Another great QuickBooks app is Salesforce. Salesforce lets you connect your customer relationship management and accounting systems to track your company's performance and pinpoint opportunities for development. The Salesforce Connector by QuickBooks is a paid product that is only available to QuickBooks Online Advanced subscribers. In order to ensure data consistency across invoices, payments, and accounts, it's great for encouraging cooperation between your finance and sales departments. Data including as invoices, sales orders, expenses, and customer information may also be shared between these two teams. Combining these two systems gives you complete insight into your business and financial flow. Using real-time data, the connection provides you with accurate information to promote company development.

DocuSign

An e-signature app DocuSign is the first e-signature connection to be added to our library of Premium Apps. The DocuSign eSignature Connector for QuickBooks Online Professional helps teams find signatures from clients, employees, and other specialists as required. DocuSign eSignature makes it simple to sign, exchange, and manage digital documents directly from QuickBooks Online Advanced. DocuSign e-Signature for QuickBooks Online Advanced allows you to submit an estimate for an electronic signature directly from QuickBooks, which will streamline operations for both you and your customers. This connection is only available to QuickBooks Online Advanced subscribers.

The Fathom

Fathom, a crucial QuickBooks plugin for small and medium-sized businesses, examines cash flow, profitability, and other performance metrics to evaluate the state of your company. As you utilize the Fathom app, you will see visuals of business intelligence data and trends that include both the financial and non-financial elements of your company. Once you are aware, you may make plans and strategies to deal with any issues directly. Even better, QuickBooks Online Advanced users get a complimentary subscription to Fathom as part of their monthly Advanced membership.

Expensify

Expensify is one of the best QuickBooks add-ons, and for good reason. Employees just need to click a button to use Expensify to expense purchases. By taking a photo of any receipt, whether it is for petrol or a client lunch, and sending it to a business credit card, employees may have their expenditure promptly authorized. Expensify's SmartScan technology extracts the merchant's name, dates, and cost amounts, then inserts the information into QuickBooks for easy and rapid verification. Paper invoices are no longer kept on file for lengthy periods of time. Expensify can handle your administrative duties, monitor your expenditures, and create a receipt bank to assist you in improving your cash flow.

Integrating Shopify and other well-known products with QuickBooks Online

Shopify

In just a few minutes, link QuickBooks Online and Shopify by following our simple setup instructions. **This is a thorough piece that highlights several crucial points while guiding you through each stage of the process.**

1. **Establish a connection:** To begin, connect your applications to QuickBooks Connector (OneSaaS). If you haven't previously, you may link Shopify and QuickBooks Online by following our steps.

2. **Set Up:** By following the setup steps below, you can decide how you want your Shopify and QuickBooks Online connection to work. You must have a basic grasp of accounting in order to make sure that the integration settings are tailored to your company's operations and accounting practices.

- **Setting up your Synchronization Options is a prerequisite for starting to configure your processes. The following must be implemented:**
  - ➢ Account time zone
  - ➢ The beginning date of integrations
  - ➢ Options for email sync reports

- **You will be presented optional workflows. The tour will utilize these processes to showcase every component of the setup process.**
  - ➢ A Shopify sales invoice will be sent to QuickBooks Online.
  - ➢ Payouts from Shopify will be sent to QuickBooks Online.
  - ➢ Shopify items will be created using QuickBooks Online.
  - ➢ QuickBooks Online will send stock-level changes to Shopify.

- Log in to access your QuickBooks Online account.

- Locate and install Intuit's Shopify Connector by going to the Apps section.

+ Click "Connect."
+ You will then be sent to the Connections tab via QuickBooks Connector (OneSaaS). To connect to Shopify, click Connect.
+ A new page requesting the domain URL will show up on your screen. Next, choose Connect to Shopify.
+ Launch your Shopify account and sign in. Your Shopify account is now linked to your approved QuickBooks Connector file.

Footnote: By selecting Add Connection, you may either add another connection or continue customizing your integration.

Workflow for creating invoices using Shopify

When you choose the When an Order is made in Shopify, produce a Sale in QuickBooks Online method, you will be presented with a prompt.

+ Configure the filters to determine which orders will be retrieved from Shopify. The order state must be followed while configuring the filters.
+ Furthermore, you have the option to record the sale in QuickBooks Online as an invoice or a sales receipt.
+ Select the Default Products and Advanced Options.
+ You will be presented with the tax setup page. Here, you must choose the QuickBooks Online tax code that matches each Shopify-created tax.
+ Furthermore, you may choose how your Shopify and QuickBooks Online goods are paired. It is possible to match by name or SKU. For sales to properly communicate with your accounting system, we need each Shopify item you have put up to have a distinct SKU.
+ Furthermore, if you want the new products that are included in your Shopify invoices to also be generated in QuickBooks Online, just tick the box next to the "Create New Items in QuickBooks Online" option. In this area, you must choose which income and cost accounts will be utilized for your inventory and non-inventory products.
+ Next, by selecting the Send Payments from Shopify to QuickBooks Online options, you can decide whether you want payment details from Shopify to be connected to your sales in QuickBooks Online.
+ The Advanced Options option allows you to connect different payment methods to different clearing accounts.
+ You also have the opportunity to create credit notes in QuickBooks Online. In this approach, you will need to map a fallback account from which the payment money is refunded. You will also need to enter your selected Refund Number Prefix, which will appear before the refund receipt number. Note: Choose the

Refunded and Partially Refunded status on the order filter in order to sync credit notes to your accounting system.

⬇ You may use the interface to link Shopify fees to QuickBooks Online invoices as expenses.

Shopify and payouts sync workflow

When you activate the payments procedure, you allow QuickBooks Connector to automatically generate deposits in QuickBooks Online for payouts that Shopify delivers to your account.

Footnote: If you want payments to sync with QuickBooks Online, you need turn off the orders workflow mentioned above. Your reported revenue might treble if this routine is set up improperly.

⬇ QuickBooks will now input your Shopify payments here as a bank transaction if you map the field "Into Bank Account." You must use either a "Bank" account or a "Other Current Asset" account. You will choose the designated account from the chart of accounts when you see your deposit in your QuickBooks Online account.

⬇ **To see the deposits that are made in QuickBooks Online:**
  ➢ From the Accounting menu, choose the Chart of Accounts.
  ➢ Select Account Assigned from the "Into Bank Account" menu.

⬇ In the Create a Deposit section, you will be asked to map the default payment method. You may choose an account here if you would like QuickBooks Connector to utilize a single clearing account for deposits from all payment methods.

Workflow for creating products

If QuickBooks Online is to produce all of your new Shopify products, choose When a Product is created on Shopify, and construct new Items in QuickBooks Online process. You have to decide which revenue and spending accounts to employ for your inventoried and non-invented items. Note: QuickBooks can only allocate the COGS account for items at the time of creation; it will not sync the COGS pricing of goods with QuickBooks Connector. Remember to save your work once you're finished.

Workflow for stock updates

Selecting the When Stock Levels are amended in QuickBooks Online, update stock levels in Shopify process option will ask you to choose the store location where the stock should be altered, as well as how you want to match the goods to QuickBooks Online items—by name or SKU.

Reminder: You should only use this option if you have stock levels set up in QuickBooks Online prior to the connection. If you don't, you risk losing all of your Shopify stock levels.

Smooth Import and Export of Data

Bringing in information from spreadsheets or other programs

Changing the management style of your company may seem like a big move. By using Excel to import your data from another software into QuickBooks, you may get up and running faster. Learn what data you can import into QuickBooks Online and how to do it to get started right away. You may manually import your current lists (suppliers, customers, products and services, and chart of accounts) into QuickBooks using Excel CSV files. You can also import your opening balance and invoices from other programs.

How to load data into QuickBooks Online

- Launch QuickBooks Online, and then sign in.
- Select Import data after going to Settings.
- Select the data that you want to import.

Reminder: After selecting a data type, you have the option to download an example file. This will help you format your data correctly.

Each Excel spreadsheet should be imported in the following sequence to guarantee correct data importation:

- Chart of Accounts
- Customer
- Suppliers
- Products and services
- Invoices
- Bills

Bring in your accounting chart

The account number, account type, account name, and detail type may all be imported into QuickBooks Online from an Excel CSV file.

1. **Format your spreadsheet:** Your chart of accounts may be imported using an Excel CSV file. Use these formatting guidelines to import your spreadsheet into QuickBooks.

- Create a new accounts spreadsheet or open your existing one.
- Make sure that the following columns are included in your spreadsheet:

- ➢ Name of Account
- ➢ Type
- ➢ Type of Detail
- ➢ The number
- ♣ If you organize your accounts by number, add a column for the account number. You may disregard this if you don't use account numbers.
- ♣ If you have more than one currency account, add a Currency column. Note: You must have enabled multi-currency in order to import and create accounts using a different currency. Multi-currency support is only available in QuickBooks Online Essentials or Plus; if you don't utilize several currencies, leave this option off.
- ♣ Subaccount: main account is how you should put a sub-account in the Account Name field if you have one. Gas, for example, is a utility. The table below provides further formatting examples for sub-accounts.
- ♣ If everything seems to be in order, save your spreadsheet in either Excel or CSV format.

2. Submit your spreadsheet
- ♣ Launch QuickBooks Online, and then sign in.
- ♣ Select Settings []. Then choose Import Data.
- ♣ Select the Chart of Accounts by clicking on it.
- ♣ Select the file to upload from your computer by clicking Browse. Then choose Open.
- ♣ Press Next.

3. Convert the fields in your spreadsheet to those in QuickBooks: To guarantee a correct import, map your accounts after uploading your spreadsheet.
- ♣ Make sure the names match the fields in QuickBooks Online by selecting the "Your Field" option.
  - ➢ Type of Detail
  - ➢ Name of Account
  - ➢ Account number
  - ➢ Type
  - ➢ The currency
- ♣ Except for Account Name, you may choose No Match if a field in your spreadsheet does not have a corresponding column. If account numbers are not utilized, for example.
- ♣ Press Next.

4. Bring your accounting chart in.
- ♣ You're almost finished. Before importing your accounts, do one last check.

- If you haven't previously, be sure to include account and detail kinds. Suggestion: Give account type correction first priority. Next, determine which kind of details is relevant to the transactions you want to keep an eye on.
- To see what needs to be repaired, move your cursor over any field that has been highlighted in red.
- You may uncheck any accounts you don't want saved.
- If everything seems to be in order, click Import.

Data exporting for analysis and stakeholder sharing

By exporting data from QuickBooks Online, users may quickly extract and use their company and financial data for a range of reporting and analytical requirements. It provides useful information for informed decision-making and makes it simple for individuals and businesses to transfer their accounting data to other software applications or systems. QuickBooks Online users may export data, such as invoices, expenses, client information, and more, in a few simple steps. By using the built-in export features in QuickBooks Online, users can ensure that their data is ready in pertinent file formats, such as Excel, CSV, or PDF, to enable smooth data management processes and platform integration.

Exporting Transactions

When exporting transactions from QuickBooks online, you must access the transaction records via the web platform in order to use the export functionality to generate the necessary data files.
- After connecting into your QuickBooks Online account, choose the specific transactions you want to export from the Transactions page.
- Next, click the "Export" button and choose your favorite file type, such Excel or CSV. After you choose the format, the system will prompt you to store the file to your local device's desired location. You may quickly obtain your financial data for any further reporting or analytical requirements with this simple process.

Report Exporting

- To export reports from QuickBooks Online, utilize the reporting options via the online platform.
- Next, produce useful data files in the formats of your choosing by selecting the appropriate export choices.

Through this process, businesses may extract valuable operational and financial data that will enable them to analyze cash flow, trends, and overall performance. By exporting reports from QuickBooks, users may utilize the data to make educated choices, forecast future outcomes, and identify potential areas for development. Important information may be shared and presented more easily within the organization when reports can be exported in many formats, such Excel or PDF.

Using Automation Tools to Increase Productivity

Streamlining processes using automation applications

The "one and done" method is no longer useful when choosing new software, and it is almost difficult to find standalone technologies that fulfill all of a user's needs in today's linked environment. Because technology cannot be "everything for everyone," third-party apps have become more common in the market. Applications from third parties are made to work with current goods and enhance their functionality. QuickBooks Online (QBO) third-party apps provide both customers and accountants with a number of advantages. By streamlining processes, reducing human labor, and reducing mistakes, automation solutions may significantly increase corporate productivity. Businesses may simplify their financial management processes by integrating QuickBooks Online with a variety of automation tools. **The automation tools listed below may assist in streamlining certain QuickBooks online workflows:**

- Use tools like InvoiceSherpa or Bill.com to prepare and distribute invoices automatically. These programs may generate bills based on pre-established schedules and templates.
- Utilize programs like QuickBooks Payments or Chaser to remind customers to make their recurring payments. Cash flow may be improved by using these methods to follow up on past-due bills.
- Use the Square, PayPal, or Stripe applications to process payments from inside QuickBooks Online. These connectors provide precise transaction recording and faster payment processing.
- Use applications like Receipt Bank or Expensify to automate the process of recording and categorizing costs. These apps enable you to scan receipts with a mobile device, automatically extracting and categorizing data.
- Use ApprovalMax or similar software to set up automated expenditure approval procedures. By ensuring that costs are reviewed and authorized in accordance with defined rules, this enhances control and compliance.
- Payroll software such as TSheets or Gusto may be used to automate payroll calculations, direct payments, and tax withholdings. You may use these

applications to sync employee data and payroll information with QuickBooks Online.

+ Make use of programs like TradeGecko or SOS Inventory to automate inventory monitoring and modifications. Inventory levels may be synchronized between QuickBooks Online and these apps.

+ Use programs like Spotlight Reporting and Fathom to automate the creation of financial reports. Personalized reports may be generated by these applications based on your schedule and specific requirements.

+ Use dashboard software like Jirav or LivePlan to create real-time financial dashboards with actionable information and visualizations.

+ Customer data may be synchronized between QuickBooks Online and CRM applications such as Salesforce or HubSpot. This ensures that customer information is up to date across all platforms.

+ Make advantage of AI-powered programs like as Pleo or QuickBooks' integrated AI capabilities to get predictive insights into cash flow, spending tendencies, and sales patterns.

Examining unique API access integrations

Businesses may add features beyond what is included in the basic package, create custom integrations, and modify processes using QuickBooks Online's extensive API (Application Programming Interface) access. Through bespoke connections, businesses may connect QuickBooks Online to their own applications, systems, and processes, resulting in enhanced efficiency and productivity. A set of guidelines and development resources is known as an application programming interface (API). The QuickBooks Online API allows developers to programmatically work with QuickBooks data and provides access to many of the features of QuickBooks, including spending, billing, payments, reporting, and customer management. It should be mentioned that QuickBooks Online has a developer site that includes comprehensive documentation, SDKs (Software Development Kits), example scripts, and API references. The documentation provides a detailed description of every endpoint—specific path—that the API may use to connect to QuickBooks data, such as /customers, /invoices, and /payments. **To configure the API access, do the actions listed below:**

+ To sign up as an Intuit Developer, visit developer.intuit.com.

+ After signing in, create a new app on the developer site. This software's function is to interface with QuickBooks Online.

+ When you build an app, you will be assigned a Client ID and Client Secret, which are necessary for authentication.

- The redirect URIs for your application is the endpoints to which users will be routed after authentication.

Keep in mind that the QuickBooks Online API uses OAuth 2.0 for login and permission. To get an access token, users must be directed to an Intuit login page. Once authentication is successful, you will be able to perform API requests on the user's behalf.

Practice Exercises

- Recognizing add-ons and app integration.
- Link Spotify and QuickBooks.
- Bring in data from Excel.
- To simplify productivity, use automation programs.

CHAPTER SEVEN
DEBUGGING AND ASSISTANCE

Recognizing and Addressing Typical Problems

Solving typical mistakes and problems

Despite QuickBooks Online's many features, users may sometimes encounter errors or malfunctions. **Some common problems and solutions are as follows:**

- **Problems with the login:** when you can't get into your QuickBooks Online account. Take the following actions to resolve this problem:
  - ➤ Make sure you are using the correct login and password by checking your credentials. If you are unable to remember your password, you may reset it by clicking the 'Forgot Password' link.
  - ➤ **Issues pertaining to browsers:** Try switching to a new browser or deleting the cookies and cache in your current one.
  - ➤ Stability of the internet connection is an important factor to take into account.
  - ➤ **Intuit Status:** Check the Intuit status page to see if there are any outages or ongoing maintenance.
- **Feeds from banks are not updating:** Transactions from banks are not synchronizing correctly.
  - ➤ By clicking on the 'Update' button beneath the Banking tab, you may manually update the bank feeds.
  - ➤ **Reconnect Bank Account:** Unplug the bank account, then plug it back in.
  - ➤ **Bank Maintenance:** Get in touch with your bank to see whether they are undergoing maintenance.
  - ➤ **Clear Cache:** Empty your browser's cache and cookies.
- **Error 108: Bank's Website Problem:** When trying to update bank feeds, you run into Error 108.
  - ➤ **Log in to your bank account:** Check your bank's website for any notifications or alerts that need your attention.
  - ➤ **Handle Issues:** Take care of any issues and follow any instructions that your bank has provided.
  - ➤ **Manual reload:** After responding to the alerts, return to QuickBooks Online and manually reload the bank feeds.
- Reports that indicate that the data is inaccurate or that some information is missing are referred to as erroneous reports.
  - ➤ **Date Range:** Verify that the report's date range is appropriately configured.

- ➤ **Criteria:** Check and adjust the report's criteria to ensure that all relevant data is included.
- ➤ **Account Setup:** Confirm that each account is properly configured and classified in the chart of accounts.
- ➤ **Balance reconciliation:** Verify all bank and credit card balances to ensure correctness.
+ **Payroll problems occur when computations or processing go wrong.**
  - ➤ **Employee Setup:** Verify that all employee data, including tax information and pay rates, is input correctly.
  - ➤ **Tax Settings:** Make sure all tax settings are configured correctly.
  - ➤ **Update QuickBooks:** Make sure your QuickBooks Online subscription includes the most current payroll tax table revisions.
  - ➤ **Communicate with Support:** If you're still having problems, contact QuickBooks Payroll support for professional assistance.
+ **Email problems with invoices:** this happens when clients do not get invoices via email.
  - ➤ **Email Address:** Verify that the customer's email address is correct.
  - ➤ Ask the customer to check their spam or trash folder.
  - ➤ Send the invoice once again, and ensure that QuickBooks provides you with a confirmation.
  - ➤ **Email setup:** Make sure QuickBooks Online's email setup settings are set up correctly.
+ **Problem with Data Sync with Third-Party Apps:** Integrated third-party apps are experiencing issues with data syncing.
  - ➤ **Check Integration Settings:** Ensure that the third-party software is linked properly and that the integration settings are right.
  - ➤ Update Apps: Make sure the most current versions of QuickBooks Online and the third-party software have been installed.
  - ➤ **Reauthorize Connection:** Permit QuickBooks Online and the third-party app to reconnect.
  - ➤ **Contact Support:** If issues persist, contact the help desks for QuickBooks as well as the third-party apps.
+ **Making amends Disparities:** Disparities that occur during a bank reconciliation.
  - ➤ **Validate Transactions:** Verify that each transaction has been appropriately documented and categorized.
  - ➤ **Starting Balance:** Verify that the starting balance in QuickBooks and your bank statement match.
  - ➤ **Uncleared Transactions:** Identify and correct any unclear transactions.

- ➢ **Manual Adjustment:** Make the required manual adjustments if needed. Just make sure you take notice of and understand the reasoning for the change.
- ✚ **Error codes:** the different error codes and their potential fixes are shown here.
  - ➢ An issue with the corporate file is indicated by the error code 6000, -77. Verify that the file is not corrupted, that it is on a local disk, and that you have the necessary rights to view it.
  - ➢ QuickBooks generates error 179 when it is unable to connect to the bank. Go to your bank's website and log in to resolve any issues.
  - ➢ A common banking mistake is 9999. In QuickBooks Online, detach and rejoin your bank account. If the issue persists, contact support.

Here are some general troubleshooting pointers:
- ✚ **Clear your cache and cookies:** This frequently resolves issues with synchronization and loading.
- ✚ **Check your connection to the internet:** Ensure that your internet connection is dependable.
- ✚ **Make a QuickBooks update:** Verify that QuickBooks Online and any integrations are using the most current versions.
- ✚ Make sure your browser is up to date and use one of the supported browsers (Chrome, Firefox, or Safari).
- ✚ If your issue continues, use Intuit's support resources, including the help center, community forums, and direct customer service.

Solutions for troubles with data sync and connection

If there is a time synchronization issue between your QuickBooks Time and QuickBooks Online accounts, QuickBooks makes every effort to determine the cause. In certain cases, you may need to search the sync log of QuickBooks Time for the answer. **To see the history of sync:**
- ✚ Go to Time > Overview > or sign in to QuickBooks Time. Navigate to QuickBooks Online's traditional QuickBooks Time.
- ✚ From the QuickBooks dropdown menu, choose View Sync Log.

Correct a payroll mapping issue

Prior to synchronizing payroll hours, each employee's payment method has to be added. **The following issues will show up if certain payment types are not set up or mapped:**
- ✚ In the QuickBooks Online interface: One of your staff members is having trouble setting up. To ensure that they are paid correctly, you must modify their pay types.

- The QuickBooks Time sync log indicates that the user has no allocated payroll items: Hours are not synchronized. Resync the time after using the Payroll Item Mapping Tool to assign payroll items to this user.

You must first add a pay type to QuickBooks Online. If you haven't previously, make sure your pay types are set up and assigned to workers in QuickBooks Online.

- Select Employees under Payroll in QuickBooks Online.
- Select a staff member.
- Under Pay types, choose Edit or Start.
- Choose which pay types are applicable.
- When you're finished, choose Save.

You may then designate payroll items in QuickBooks Time by selecting Preferences from the QuickBooks dropdown menu under QuickBooks Time after completing the aforementioned configuration.

- Select the choice for the Payroll Item Mapping Tool.
- Choose the kind of compensation for each employee.
- When finished, close the window.

Resolve a closure date issue

The books in your QuickBooks business file are closed for the time that has to be transferred when you try to sync time with QuickBooks Online and run into one of the following issues.

You could notice one of the following errors:

- QuickBooks Online issue while exporting X hours, error code: 6200, QuickBooks detail: The account's time period is over.
- As per the QuickBooks time sync log, the timesheet was rejected with the following explanation: "An attempt was made to modify a Time Tracking with a date that is on or before the company's closing date." Error Code 6200 Details: The account term has finished.

Here are several solutions to remedy this:

- In QuickBooks Online, choose Settings ⬚, followed by Accounts and settings.
- Select Advanced to modify the books' closure date, then click Save in the Accounting section.

Resolve a feature issue

When you try to sync in QuickBooks Time, you will get the message "Insufficient Permissions" OR "Permission Denied" because you do not have the required rights in QuickBooks Online to perform this activity. You must either contact your admin or log in as the primary admin to QuickBooks Time or QuickBooks Online in order to upgrade your permissions.

Resolve a missing employee issue

An employee's name in QuickBooks Time and QuickBooks Online must exactly match in order to export hours. Your sync log will show the message "Can't export [employee's] time, because the user's account isn't found in your QuickBooks Employee List" if they don't. The answer to this is as follows: Employee names in QuickBooks Time and QuickBooks Online must exactly match for hours to sync. Your sync log will show the message "Can't export [employee's] time, because the user's account isn't found in your QuickBooks Employee List" if they don't. **The answer to this is as follows:**

- Click View Sync Log after selecting QuickBooks from the selection menu in QuickBooks Time.
- Click "Fix." Next to the error message is this. Select a different sync report to be sure you don't overlook the error notice. Red highlights indicate error warnings in sync reports.
- QuickBooks Online has a list of your workers. Locate and choose the right worker.

> ➤ If you can't find the employee, you'll need to add them to QuickBooks Online. Next, try matching the employee again.
> ➤ If you want to avoid synchronizing this employee's time, you may choose to omit this user's time.
> ✦ Click "Save." Repeat the procedure if more than one employee is not matched.

Resolve an authentication issue

If you get the following error notice while trying to sync hours from QuickBooks Time to QuickBooks Online, it means that the permission token from Intuit has expired: "Internal error: 3200:message=Exception authenticating OAuth; errorCode=003200; statusCode=401" . **The answer to this is as follows:**

> ✦ Close the QuickBooks Time window and
> ✦ Sign in as QuickBooks Online's principal administrator.
> ✦ Select Start QuickBooks Time after navigating to Time.

> ✦ Examine a different synchronization.

Using Online Help for QuickBooks

Official channels and resources for assistance

1. Speak with Support
> ✦ Open the QuickBooks Online account for your business.
> ✦ Select Help (?).

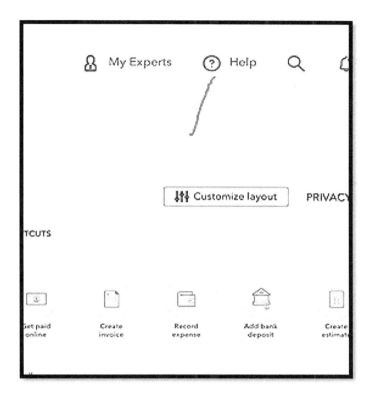

+ **Select one of the tabs to get started.**
  - ➢ **Assistant:** Get timely, customized answers. You may either choose one of the recommended alternatives or enter in a query or problem you need assistance with. If you decide you need more help, you can still talk to a human.
  - ➢ **Search:** Click Contact Us to select a way to contact us, or perform a direct search using the QuickBooks Online knowledge base:
    - ❖ To speak with a help specialist, open a chat window.
    - ❖ Ask the expert who is next available for a callback.
    - ❖ Ask businesses like yours to help the community.

Discussion boards and professional guidance

If you have any questions about QuickBooks or anything else pertaining to business or practice, join the QuickBooks Community! There, you can network with experts and peers. Please feel free to ask questions, get answers, and share ideas, advice, and more.
Here's the method:
  + Go to QuickBooks Community.
  + After logging in, choose QuickBooks Community.

158

- Choose QuickBooks Q&A.
- Next to QuickBooks Q & A, there is a dropdown option. Select your QuickBooks product from there.
- Once a subject has been chosen, click "Start a debate."
- Click Post after adding a topic and your question or discussion point.

Utilizing tutorials, webinars, and guides for help

Gaining competence with QuickBooks Online may considerably increase your ability to manage your money. QuickBooks offers a number of products, including webinars, seminars, and manuals, to help users in getting the most of their application. **Here are some tips for maximizing these resources:**

QuickBooks Online Tutorials

Below are things you get to learn using QuickBooks online;
- **Step-by-Step Guide:** Comprehensive instructions on how to carry out various operations, such as handling payroll or setting up your account.
- **Video Demonstrations:** Step-by-step explanations with images that lead users through the QuickBooks Online interface.

+ **Interactive Learning:** In some lessons, you may practice tasks in a QuickBooks environment that is imitated.

You may acquire access to the tutorials using the following ways;
+ **QuickBooks Help Center:** Go to the tutorials area of the QuickBooks Help Center.
+ **YouTube Channel:** QuickBooks includes a library of educational videos on its official YouTube channel.
+ **Inside-Product Support:** You may search for the problem you need assistance with by clicking on the help button and obtaining tutorials right from inside QuickBooks Online.

Webinars for QuickBooks

The benefits of attending a QuickBooks webinar are listed below:
+ **Live Sessions:** Participate in live webinars hosted by QuickBooks experts. These presentations include a Q&A section where you may ask specific questions.
+ **Webinars that were recorded:** Watch webinars that have already been recorded so you may learn at your own pace.
+ **Focused Topics:** Webinars cover a broad variety of topics, from basic setup and navigation to more complex features like payroll and tax administration.

To access the previously described content, do the actions listed below:
+ **This is the QuickBooks website:** Visit the QuickBooks website to see previously recorded sessions or sign up for future webinars.
+ **Email notifications:** To be informed about upcoming webinars and events, sign up for QuickBooks' email updates.
+ **Additional Service Suppliers:** QuickBooks Online seminars are also offered by a few accounting firms and business advisors.

Practice Exercises

+ Recognize and Solve Typical Problems regarding QuickBooks online
+ Discuss the means of accessing Online Help for QuickBooks

CHAPTER EIGHT

INDUSTRIAL APPLICATIONS AND PRACTICAL USE SCENARIOS

Small Business QuickBooks Online

Real-world experiences and success accounts

Airbnb: The sharing economy's peer-to-peer renting marketplace

By making it easier for travelers to rent private rooms or homes for a short period of time, Airbnb revolutionized the lodging brokerage sector. The website functions as a marketplace where landlords may post their offerings and tourists can discover suitable housing. Because of this, Airbnb is radically changing the conventional hotel industry and making it possible for tourists to enjoy more personalized and affordable overnight stays. Additionally, the company offers ordinary citizens an easy way to make money off of their living space. Technology-wise, Airbnb runs an intuitive website and app that handles bookings, payments, and reviews. Its effectiveness has mostly been ascribed to reducing security concerns and promoting mutual trust between strangers. With operations in over 100,000 places worldwide, Airbnb is now among the most valuable companies. Airbnb has had a huge impact on the sharing economy and transformed a whole online industry with its innovative peer-to-peer model for short-term private rentals.

Zalando: The e-commerce fashions retailer

Zalando quickly became the biggest online fashion retailer in Europe, revolutionizing the way consumers buy for clothes. Customers can simply choose from hundreds of styles on Zalando and have them delivered to their homes, saving them the trouble of walking from shop to store. Delivery times might be as short as one or two days thanks to large storage facilities and transportation hubs. Zalando gives businesses and designers an easy way to reach a large online audience. At the same time, shoppers may find new fashions and be inspired. Zalando, a fully online business, uses modern payment methods and personalization to ease every step of online sales. Large selection, great ease, and a strong brand are the cornerstones of this successful e-commerce firm approach. By introducing and refining online clothes shopping, Zalando is completing the digital transformation of an entire sector. By consistently focusing on the needs of its online customers, Zalando has swiftly emerged as the industry leader.

Uber: The On-Demand Economy's Ridesharing Company

Uber's ride-sharing service transformed urban transportation and filled a market void. The program connects drivers and passengers and enables cooperative usage of private automobiles with a simple finger touch. While drivers have a simple method to earn additional money, passengers benefit from less priced, more flexible travel. With the use of GPS, maps, and payment methods, Uber's technology is based on direct smartphone mediation. Success aspects include simplicity of use, cost savings compared to taxis, and rapid availability. Drivers' working conditions and the confusing regulatory environment have been criticized on occasion. When everything is said and done, Uber is a good example of how a smart digital business plan can disrupt a mature sector. Uber's innovative idea of using technology to coordinate the use of private resources has completely changed transportation throughout the world. The on-demand economy is a notion that may be applied to various sectors and has served as an inspiration for many other enterprises.

Netflix: The streaming service with a subscription model

By offering online streaming services for movies and TV shows, Netflix revolutionized the media sector. For a monthly fee, Netflix provides its customers with basic on-demand watching across many devices as well as access to an ever-growing library of films. Through in-house productions, the streaming service creates unique content and brands that maintain consumer engagement. Recommendation engines discover new content in addition to providing personalized suggestions. Netflix often uses analytics and big data to enhance its offerings and user experience. The startup is steadily displacing linear television and posing a severe threat to established broadcasters. A major change in the business has been brought about by Netflix, which has completely changed the way people watch videos. With its ground-breaking streaming approach that bundles convenience, a wide selection, and customization into a single subscription, Netflix has raised the bar and established norms in the video industry.

Spotify: The freemium music streaming service

With its music streaming services, Spotify has radically changed the music business and listening patterns. A large music collection is available for users to listen on demand and create their own playlists. Musicians may engage and connect directly with audiences using Spotify. The business concept is based on paid premium memberships with additional features and advertising. Finding new artists is one of the service's primary benefits, along with personalization and simplicity of use. Thanks to partnerships with IT teams, Spotify can be simply integrated into devices. With more music being streamed than purchased, Spotify is spearheading the digital transformation of the music business. For record labels, this means whole new types of partnerships and income streams. Spotify's innovative use of the Internet to provide music on demand has altered customer behavior. Digital distribution, data analytics, and personalized suggestions are crucial in today's music industry. Spotify is a prime illustration of how digital business tactics can update established companies.

Amazon: The Cloud Computing and E-Commerce Giant (cloud services, e-commerce)

Amazon began as an online bookstore before expanding to become the world's largest e-commerce company. These days, the huge online store offers a large assortment, simple delivery options (like Prime), and a high degree of purchasing and payment ease. Over time, Amazon changed the retail industry and became one of the first companies to run entirely online. Logistics innovations, such as its own network of shipping centers, allow Amazon to deliver items quickly and reliably. Amazon established a whole new market segment for cloud infrastructure and digital services for business customers with AWS. AWS is now the leading provider of cloud computing solutions worldwide and a driving factor behind the digitalization of businesses. Amazon has successfully used cloud computing and online retailing to carve out a unique niche for itself. The company skillfully demonstrates how long-term success can be achieved by technical innovation, entrepreneurial vision, and a continual emphasis on the demands of the customer. Amazon is among the greatest illustrations of how old industries are being transformed by digital business methods.

Tesla: The direct-to-consumer producer of electric vehicles

As a leader in electric mobility, Tesla increased the general market's adoption of sustainable powertrain technology. By producing e-cars that were highly innovative, visually beautiful, and targeted, Tesla shattered the paradigm for electric transportation. Features like software integration, digital updates, and driver assistance systems set Tesla's cars apart. By selling directly via its shops and online, Tesla eliminates dealer profits and is able to provide e-cars at a lower price. The company's network of Superchargers offers convenient and fast charging while on the road. A major factor in the mobility revolution is Tesla's production of fashionable but useful electric cars. For other manufacturers, Tesla serves both a model and a disruptive competitor. Tesla has shown that eco-friendly innovations can be profitable by consistently highlighting digital technology and e-mobility. The business effectively illustrates how digital services, technical leadership, and direct customer interaction can disrupt established businesses.

Google: The ad-supported search engine and advertising platform

With billions of queries answered every day, Google is the most widely used search engine. The effectiveness of Google's search algorithm is essential to its growth and success. The bulk of Google's income comes from targeted text and image ads that are linked to website content and search terms. Google created Android; the most widely used smartphone operating system globally. Because of its vast ecosystem, which encompasses search, advertising, mobile, video, maps, and more, the tech giant dominates the digital economy and a sizable chunk of the Internet. Emerging products like Google Assistant, a voice assistant, are built on AI and data. Google has become the hub of the digital age by revolutionizing the way people engage with information. Google's business strategy is a remarkable example of how user data, targeted advertising, and state-of-the-art technology can combine to create a quickly expanding and very lucrative company.

Lessons from successful companies

Being an entrepreneur is a journey filled with successes and failures, highs and lows. Many of the world's most successful businesspeople have experienced both. You could discover a lot about the things that some of today's most prominent businesspeople, such as Elon Musk, Oprah Winfrey, and Jeff Bezos, wish they had understood before launching their companies. These are some key lessons that may inspire and guide aspiring business entrepreneurs.

Jeff Bezos: The Influence of Strategic Planning

The founder of Amazon has changed how people read, purchase, and even watch TV in addition to becoming one of the largest e-commerce websites in the world. However, he acknowledges that the most crucial talent he acquired was the capacity for long-term thinking. Bezos advises prospective entrepreneurs to focus on their long-term objectives. He emphasizes that instead than becoming distracted by short-term financial gain, entrepreneurs should concentrate on creating long-term value. His own experience with Amazon, which suffered years of losses before becoming the biggest e-commerce firm in the world, is in line with this remark.

Oprah Winfrey: The Value of Genuineness

Oprah Winfrey, a media tycoon, TV host, and philanthropist, attributes her success to being herself. Sincere and genuine individuals, in her opinion, are relatable. When launching a business, Oprah counsels prospective entrepreneurs to be true to their brand and themselves. This means not trying to be someone they're not and being truthful with their audience. Being genuine may help build trust and connections, two things that are crucial for building a powerful brand.

Elon Musk: The Importance of Adaptability

Elon Musk, the founder of SpaceX and Tesla, has a history of running into a lot of problems in his commercial endeavors. He regrets not understanding the value of resilience from the beginning. Musk asserts that becoming an entrepreneur is not for the faint of heart. It often involves failure, censure, and tremendous stress. He highlights how important resilience is in these circumstances. Musk believes that future entrepreneurs should be prepared to endure losses, adapt to change, and never give up. Perseverance and a strong commitment to your objective may make all the difference.

In addition to the lessons that Elon Musk, Oprah Winfrey, and Jeff Bezos have taught, potential entrepreneurs might benefit from the following general viewpoints:

- **Accept Failure:** Be open to the possibility of failing since it often acts as a launching pad for success. Mistakes provide us priceless lessons that may inspire innovation and growth.
- **Adaptability:** In today's rapidly changing world, the ability to adapt is crucial. Entrepreneurs should be flexible in changing their direction as necessary.
- **Lifelong Learning:** Being an entrepreneur is a continuous process. Keep learning, be curious, and seek out knowledge from a variety of sources.
- **Sturdy Network:** Create a strong network of advisors, mentors, and peers who can provide guidance, criticism, and motivation.
- **Purpose and Enthusiasm:** Pursue business ventures that align with your passions and ideals. A genuine sense of purpose in life may serve as a powerful motivator.

Practice Exercises

- Discuss few Real-world experiences and success accounts
- Discuss some lessons you have learnt from successful companies

The Appendices

A glossary of words and meanings to make things easier to grasp

A

- **Accounts Payable (A/P):** The sum of money that a company owes its vendors or suppliers for goods and services that it has received. The 'costs' area in QuickBooks Online is where costs are controlled.
- **A/R, or accounts receivable,** is the money that customers owe a business for products and services rendered. Sales are managed using the 'Sales' tab in QuickBooks Online.
- **Assets:** Assets are resources possessed by a firm that have a monetary value, such money, stock, machinery, and real estate.

B

- **Balance Sheet:** A financial statement that shows the assets, liabilities, and equity of a business at a certain point in time.
- **Bank reconciliation:** This is the process of reconciling the information on a company's bank statement with the balances in its accounting records.
- **Bill:** A bill is a document that documents the amount owed to a vendor or supplier and the business purchase.

C

- **Cash flow** is the total amount of money coming into and going out of a firm, especially as it relates to liquidity.
- **Chart of Accounts (COA):** An inventory of all accounts used in an organization's accounting system, arranged according to income, cost, liability, and asset.
- **Cost of Goods Sold (COGS):** The upfront expenses related to producing the products that a business sells such labor and materials.

D

- **Deposit:** Funds deposited into a bank account, often recorded in QuickBooks Online during customer payments.
- **Double-Entry Accounting:** An accounting system that follows the equation assets = liabilities + equity and in which every transaction impacts a minimum of two accounts.

E

- **Equity:** Equity is calculated by subtracting liabilities from assets and represents the owner's wish for the company. Common stock, retained profits, and other equity accounts are included in this.

+ **Expense:** The costs a business incurs while generating income, including office supplies, rent, utilities, and wages.

F

+ **Financial Statements:** These reports, which include the balance sheet, income statement, and cash flow statement, describe the financial performance and position of an organization.

I

+ **Income Statement (Profit and Loss Statement):** A financial report that shows the sales, expenses, and profits or losses of a business over a certain time period.
+ **Invoice:** An invoice is a document that a company sends to its customers that lists the goods or services rendered together with the total amount due.

J

+ **Journal Entry:** In the accounting system, a journal entry is a record of a financial transaction that contains the date, amounts, affected accounts, and a short description.

L

+ **Liability:** Examples of obligations that firms owe to other parties are mortgages, loans, and accounts payable.
+ **Liquidity:** The quick ratio or current ratio shows a company's ability to meet its short-term commitments.

P

+ **Payroll:** Payroll is the process of sending money, calculating wages, and withholding taxes for workers.
+ **Purchase Order (PO):** A document that outlines the kind, amount, and agreed-upon price of goods or services that a buyer gives to a seller

R

+ Reconciliation is the process of verifying the consistency of two sets of data, usually the balances of two accounts.
+ **Recurring Transaction:** QuickBooks Online allows for the automation of recurring transactions, which include monthly rent or subscription payments.

S

+ **Sales Receipt:** This document serves as proof of sale and documentation of money received at the time of the transaction.
+ **Statement of Cash Flows:** This kind of financial document lists all of the cash inflows and outflows that occurred during a certain time period and classifies them as financing, investing, or operating activities.

T

- **Trial Balance:** A report that shows the balances of every account in the general ledger and is used to make sure that the total debits and credits are equal.
- **Transaction:** Any business transaction that affects the financial accounts monetarily is considered a transaction. This includes purchases, sales, payments, and receipts.

U

- **Undeposited Funds:** A temporary holding account for received funds before they are transferred to a bank account.

V

- **Vendor:** A vendor is an individual or company that supplies another company with products or services. You may manage suppliers in QuickBooks Online by going to the 'Expenses' page.

Final Thoughts

Its position as the leading financial management tool for companies of all sizes is further cemented with QuickBooks Online 2025. Business owners can manage their finances, streamline operations, and make informed choices because to its user-friendly design, wealth of features, and comprehensive support. The scalability of QuickBooks Online 2025 is among its most noteworthy features. Whether you run a large company with complex financial requirements or a small firm just starting out, QuickBooks Online can be tailored to meet your needs. Businesses may customize QuickBooks to fit their unique processes and industry standards thanks to its easy integration with a wide range of third-party apps. When it comes to providing advanced financial management capabilities, QuickBooks Online 2025 is excellent. It offers everything a company needs to maintain accurate financial records and provide insightful data, from thorough revenue and expense monitoring to robust inventory management and thorough reporting. Business owners can focus on expansion and strategies thanks to the platform's automation features, which remove human data input, minimize mistakes, and save time. QuickBooks Online 2025 sets itself out as a complete, adaptable, and trustworthy financial management tool. It is a terrific tool for anybody looking to enhance their financial procedures, get more financial information, and propel company success because of its constant innovation and commitment to meeting the needs of contemporary companies.

INDEX

O

N

P